TANK ANGLING

IN

INDIA

Owing to the antiquity and rarity of this book, certain pages are regrettably absent, and readability is compromised due to the blurring of the original text. If you possess any insights regarding the availability of these missing sections, kindly inform us. Your assistance is crucial in ensuring the completion of this significant work for the benefit of future generations.

TANK ANGLING

IN

INDIA.

BY

HENRY SULLIVAN THOMAS

GYAN

Published by

Gyan Publishing House
5, Ansari Road
Daryaganj, New Delhi-110002
Phone: 011-47034999, 9811692060
E-mail: books@gyanbooks.com

Distribution Network
gyanbooks.com
India, USA, Canada, UK, Australia

ISBN: 978-93-6280-665-9 (HB)
First Published, 1887

2nd Impression 2024

Printed at: Gyan Press, Delhi.

TANK ANGLING IN INDIA
Author: HENRY SULLIVAN THOMAS

TANK ANGLING.

Plate I

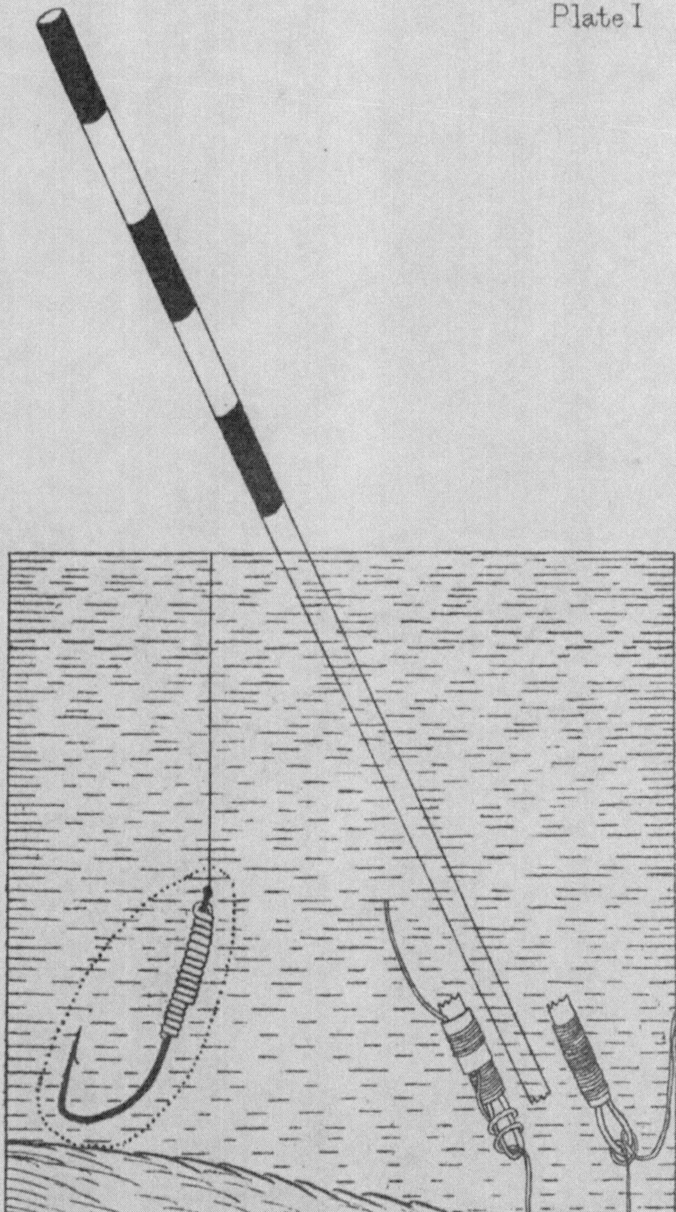

THE DETECTIVE FLOAT

TANK ANGLING

IN

INDIA.

BY

HENRY SULLIVAN THOMAS,
MADRAS CIVIL SERVICE,
F. L. S., F. Z. S.

Author of "The Rod in India," &c.

WITH ILLUSTRATIONS.

MADRAS: HIGGINBOTHAM & CO., 165, Mount Road.
By Appointment in India to H. R. H. The Prince of Wales.
LONDON: HAMILTON ADAMS & CO., 32, Paternoster Row.
1887.

Dedication.

"*Piscatoribus Sacrum.*"

Izaak Walton.

PREFACE.

"To all readers of this discourse, but especially to the honest angler."—IZAAK WALTON.

Because it is a loving and innocent fish that hurts nothing that hath life, and is at peace with all the numerous inhabitants of that vast watery element; and truly I think *most anglers are so disposed to most of mankind.*—COMPLEAT ANGLER, Part I.

"Can't you do anything for us Mr. Thomas?" I was asked by one who was tied by his profession to his stool, and had no tents or camp kit, or camp servants, or camp knowledge, or official influence to make possible a pilgrimage to the wild haunts of the Mahseer. The same appeal has been made to me by jailors, shopkeepers, and others of slender means to whom the expenses of an encampment in the jungles would be out of the question but who are none the less brothers of the angle. This appeal it is from exiled brother anglers that has impelled me to try and work out some sort of Indian fishing that would be within their reach. The result is this little volume on "Tank Angling in India."

It has also been complained to me that "*The Rod in India,*" 2nd edition is too expensive. I am sorry for it. It was my mistake in introducing superior plates by a first class artist, and other things which altogether cost me over £ 400 which has not come back again. In the interests of my poorer brethren of the angle I have aimed at making this little volume as cheap as possible. Perhaps I have rushed from Scylla into Carybdis. I must risk it, if it is only to find out how many fishermen there are in India to whom a cheap book on cheap fishing is a desideratum.

If this venture clears itself I may amuse the leisure of my retirement by bringing out a 3rd edition of "*The Rod in India*" in like cheap form, and with much added material, that is as soon as the present edition is exhausted. I may also improve this present little volume, for I count confidently on its provoking brother anglers to aid the common cause of fishing in the land of our exile. So I will repeat here the invitation made in "*The Rod in India.*"

"If brother anglers reading these pages feel inclined to give me the benefit of their further experiences, I shall hope to embody or quote them in some possible future edition. The collected wisdom of all anglers in all parts of India might thus grow into a very complete book, sufficient to show the best means of securing the best sport available in different localities in India.

"This invitation, thrown out in my first edition, has been very kindly responded to by anglers. Not a few have written to me direct, and others have contributed papers to the "*Field,*" and to the "*Asian,*" some professedly in answer to this invitation, others in the same spirit of helping fellow-fishermen to sport. For myself I beg to tender cordial acknowledgments to all who have thus helped in what I must call the kindliest manner. I am confirmed in the conviction, always fixed in my mind, that it is very rare for a good fisherman not to be a good fellow. For others, readers of this little volume, the result is happy, for they will not be confined to my ideas only, but will have the opinions and the experience of others also. Believing that my readers will be glad to have the views of others, as well as my own, and recognizing that India is too large a field for any one person to cover unaided, I have endeavoured to bring together in this volume all the information kindly afforded by others. That contained in newspaper contributions will be found in Chapter XXIV, on Fishing Localities, the source and the *nom de plume* being always given. Some of my readers may find double interest in, and attach increased weight to, these contributions, from recognizing under a *nom de plume* a friend well known by them to be a master in the art.

"Besides the contributions of unknown writers, I am able to give my readers two interesting communications, one from the pen of Colonel J. Parsons, and the other by Colonel W. Osborn, Commanding 9th M. N. I. Sportsmen will find them both valuable.

"The further experience had since 1873 has also enabled me to introduce not a little additional matter of my own.

"If sportsmen think that the above invitation has resulted in any advantage to themselves, perhaps they will allow me to renew it in this edition. Though I cannot be sanguine that this book will live to a third edition, still stranger things have happened, and it is just possible that it may again come to pass that anglers, who have put themselves to the kindly trouble of co-operating through the press or direct, may find that, in the total of experiences put together, they get more than any one of them could individually contribute.

"Anglers are in England a numerous class, whereas in India they form a very small minority of the lovers of sport. Whether for love, or for money, shooting of any sort, and more particularly heavy game shooting, is so much more difficult to obtain in England than in India, that many who in England perforce content themselves with the rod, would in India be seduced by the ruder attractions of the boar-spear, the rifle, and the gun. For myself I can well remember a day in camp "marked evermore with white," when rising at dawn I heard over my early cup of coffee the trumpeting of elephants, knew that there was a fair chance also of Bison, Sambur, and Spotted-deer, knew also that there was a Mahseer river in the valley. In one corner of the camp hut was the battery, in the other were the rods and tackle. Which shall it be? I may get up to those elephants in a quarter of an hour, I may trudge ten miles and not get a shot. I know that I can make a certainty of the Mahseer. I chose the latter, and brought home six fine fish before breakfast, and never regretted my choice. But I think there are not a few who, in like circumstances, would unhesitatingly have preferred the rifle to the rod. And thus it comes about that anglers are in India comparatively few. They are all too few to help each other adequately with information over so wide an area as India; all too few to make it worth while to write a book on the subject, except for the love of the thing, therefore there is all the more reason why they should continue to help each other as much as they can."

Still you will not expect me to bring out new editions till the present ones are sold off or nearly so. This by way of warning to a well-to-do but o'er canny Scot who told me he should wait till my revised edition came out. He may have to wait a long time, and lose many a good days fishing in the interim, and it will serve him right!

For my plates 3, 4, 10, 11, 12, 14, 15 I am indebted to photozincographic copies from Day's *Fishes of India.*

H. S. THOMAS.

MADRAS,
December, 1887.

CONTENTS.

CHAPTER I.

PASTE BAITING.

CHAPTER II.

LIVE-BAIT PICKETING.

CHAPTER III.

LIVE-BAIT WITH A FLOAT.

CHAPTER IV.

WORM AND PRAWN FISHING.

CHAPTER V.

LOCALITIES.

CHAPTER VI.

STOCKING PONDS.

CHAPTER VII.

THE MAINSPRING OF FISH-LIFE.

CHAPTER VIII.

NAMES, DESCRIPTION AND HABITAT OF FISH.

ILLUSTRATIONS.

D

TANK ANGLING IN INDIA.

CHAPTER I.

PASTE BAITING.

There we sit
For a bit
Till we fish entangle.

* * *

We sit still
And watch our quill;
Fishers must not wrangle.

JO: CHALKHILL.

It is not given to everyone to kill the mighty Mahseer, nor is it always convenient to make a pilgrimage to his haunts, so suppose we try a little bottom fishing just for a change. "Variety's charming": we have it on the old indisputable authority of the copybook. And the swan-quill is not without its charm. There it sits elegant and upright in the water, like a sprightly little water-nymph in its element, on the very tip-toe of expectation, and ready to give you the earliest hint of the slightest flirtation going on with your bait down below. You feel you have a friend in that quill, it will tell you faithfully of every move made against you in the dark depths below, and you have a conviction you may trust it implicitly. In cautious silence your little nymph makes mute gestures to you, by a code of her own, like the signs of the needle speaking to you of the man at the other end of the wire. Mind you are quick to read her aright, for your nymph is true as steel, and will tell you all, if you can only follow her signals. There! she made the slightest shade of a bow; some one has entered the room, shall we say just smelt your bait. Again she bows, curtseys, now more and more rapidly, now she is quite excited over it; in fact all of a tremor lest you should be too late. Strike instanter, not roughly, but rapidly. Ha! it's you is it? I thought as much. But mind, mind what you are about, you have only single gut, and a light rod, and seemingly a stout party at the other end. Out goes the line off the reel, not very fast certainly, nor very far, still the old alderman will have it, and there's no denying him. He fights long and persistently though not furiously, nor with the activity of youth. Stick to him, keep bearing on the old party all you dare, but gingerly, gingerly. What, no signs of my poor little faithful nymph yet, still down in the depths keeping an eye on that fat fellow? Ah, up she shows at last, one is quite glad to see her little face again. She tells you that the old alderman is getting pumped. His every instinct is to keep down at the bottom in deep water, so keep pressing on him upwards and shorewards. At last you have him in the landing net, a 7 lb. fish with a funny little fringed mouth. What is he? He is a Labeo, one of twenty-five, of which eight run large, attaining respectively to 1½ feet, 2 feet, 3 feet, and in one case to nearly 5 feet in length, according to Dr. Day. I have only the pleasure of a personal acquaintance with four of them, and they are all similarly thick-built fish, and to be taken in one and the same way. These fish being of the sizes above-mentioned, and all, as far as I know them, thick-built heavy fish for their length, anglers will see that they are worth fishing for. I have no note of having caught them over 7 lbs. with a line myself, but a friend caught two weighing 8 lbs. 4 oz. and 8 lbs. 7 oz., and I am assured by a gentleman with whom I have been fishing, and whom I thus know to be far too well acquainted with them to make any mistake of identity, I am assured by him that on one occasion he saw and weighed one of 20 lbs. The large Temple Tank at Manàrgudi, if you will have your information specific, was running so low that the fish were all

Plate II

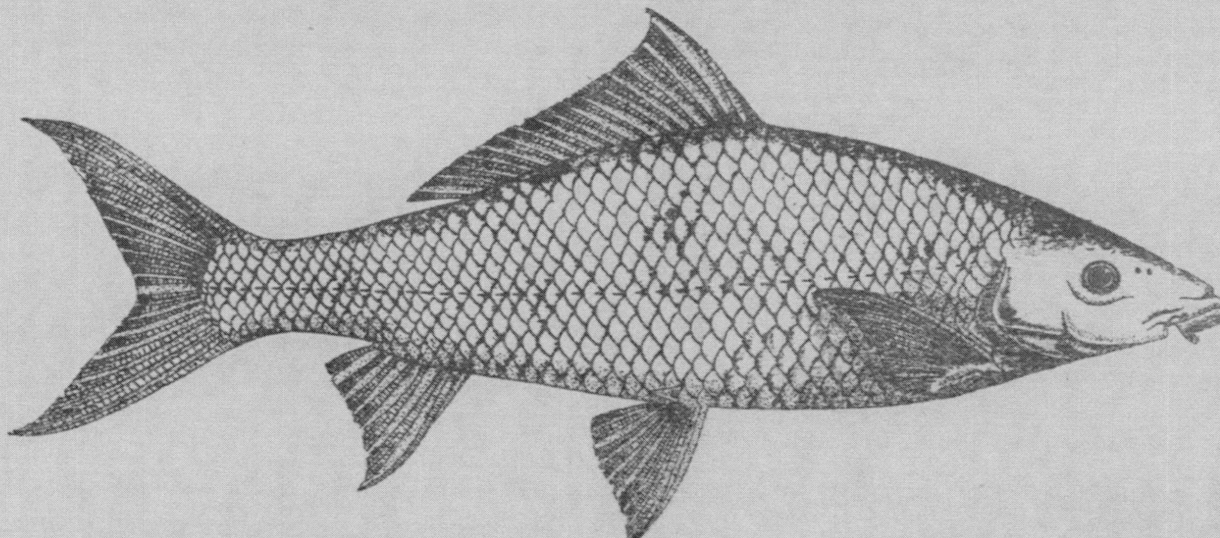

LABEO CALBASU

lying half dead on their sides, and the crowds were walking in and freely spearing them; and this one was weighed by him. Added to this I have myself seen lines freely broken, and suffered it myself.

A Labeo, let me tell you, is as cunning a fish as a roach, every bit, nay more so; much more so, and therein he will tax your skill the more severely, though he is to be fished for in much the same manner. Good roach fishing is the glory of the Londoner, and here is just the same for you with the added recommendation of being much more refinedly difficult, and with the fish seldom under 1 lb., averaging 2 lbs., and commonly running to 5 and 6 pounds, with always a possible 20 pounds in the mind's eye, as well as in the pond. I am afraid of want of sympathy for float fishing, and I must confess that I myself held it mighty cheap for many a long year, and that though I am one of those who are very much in sympathy with a gentleman who at an angling club dinner declared, in the face of all the salmon tamers present, that he would rather catch tadpoles than catch nothing. Still I am afraid of want of sympathy for float fishing for I well remember that it was some time before I cared to fish with anything but a fly. I thought that trout-taking with an artificial fly was the very acme of skill, and that once having known it I could not condescend to anything less refined. But in time the Mahseer convinced me, as I have admitted in The Rod in India, that he was to be taken both much more freely and also of a better size by spinning than by fly fishing. And then I found out that to be a first class spinner was infinitely more difficult than to be all that could be desired either with the salmon fly or even with the trout or dace fly. My old conceits were knocked out of me. And since then I have found out that to carry Labeo fishing to the perfection of skill is in some respects even more difficult than either fly fishing, or spinning for Mahseer. So you need not be in too much of a hurry to chuck the book down with an "Oh! bottom fishing! I never could be bothered with it." If you do so turn away allow me to say, it is because you do not know enough about it. The successful roach fisher looks upon all other branches of the angling art as inferior in skill to what his own requires of him, and, I stick to what I said in The Rod in India, that it is in the exhibition of skill that the element of sport consists. Till you have acquired that refinement of skill which he rejoices in you simply don't believe in him, and by the natural corollary of ignorance think you know a great deal more about it. It is the precise principle on which people come out to India for a two or three months' flit and go home again thoroughly convinced to full satisfaction point that all we who have been 20 or 30 years out here are nothing better than poor old fumblers; that they, the flitters who come in and go out with the snipe in the cold season, have got the whole thing in a nutshell, and are competent to write books on it!! And a deal of mischief they do by it. "I don't care *what* Thomas says" said an old friend of mine on a fishing point on which the dear old fellow's knowledge was not on a par with his goodness, and if you, dear reader, are in like manner inconvincibly prejudiced against bottom fishing, let me tell you you are simply ruining your prospects for life. In the still lingering hope of seducing some at least from unbelief in bottom fishing I must transgress the rule which I have ordinarily laid down for myself, and, break the promise which I made in the opening words of the preface to the first edition of The Rod in India; "I promise that "you shall not be wearied by long yarns about the fish that "I have caught; the object is to set your rod bending and "your heart leaping." But here the object is to induce you not to turn up your nose at bottom fishing, and to persuade you to give it a trial. So I trust I may stand excused if I mention a little bag made one day just to draw the reader on. A friend and self caught in a pond 21 lbs. weight

Plate III

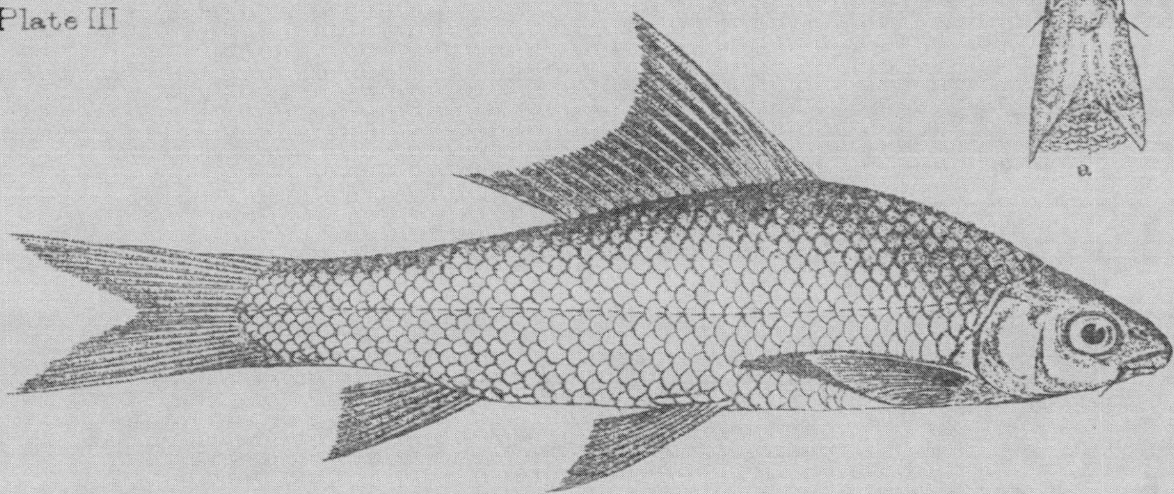

CIRRHINA CIRRHOSA

in one hour. Some of them were 3 lbs. each, but the majority were about 2 lbs. each. Another day I got 25 lbs. weight of these fish, besides two freshwater tortoises, weighing together $6\frac{1}{2}$ lbs. There were two more good fish also that a new hand broke off my hook in his clumsy hurry with the landing net (bad luck to him), and another that fairly broke me after a long fight. I suppose I thought it was about time he gave in, and he thought otherwise, for they fight long and obstinately, in brief most gamely, and my tackle was somewhat fine. Another tortoise also was hooked foul, brought to the top and lost. This fishing was from 7-10 A.M. to 10-50 A.M. During the first hour I took nothing; during the remaining two hours and 40 minutes I landed the above $31\frac{1}{2}$ lbs., on a light single-handed 10 ft. trout rod. When I left they were still biting, but I had to tear myself away. Fishing all day H caught 52 lbs., of which two were freshwater sharks, weighing respectively 10 lbs. and 22 lbs.; the rest were the fish I am introducing to you. A friend fishing with him that day caught about 30 lbs. weight, but of this I speak roughly from hearsay and estimate, not having seen his bag. Thus the two rods took about 80 lbs. weight of fish out of a pond near Negapatam.

Four rods in three days caught 678 lbs. Of these fish two were Freshwater Sharks (*Wallago attu*) of 11 lbs. each; the rest were Labeos and White Carp (*Cirrhina cirrhosa*). We also lost one Freshwater Shark which leaped four feet into the air, and by comparison with the eleven pounders looked 20 lbs. We were also broken three or four times by fish which from their manner of biting we concluded to be Labeos. Of the Labeos and White Carp which we took, and brought to scale, the majority ran 1 lb., $1\frac{1}{2}$ lbs., 2 lbs. each, while a very good sprinkling were 3, 4, 5, 6 and 7 lbs. each, and some little fellows of $\frac{1}{4}$ lb. came in out of pure cussedness for the sole purpose of spoiling our average.

I was telling a friend of this bag of 678 lbs. by 4 rods in 3 days when he said "you should send that to 'The Field.'" "It was such an unusual bag" I replied "that they would "only think I was lying." Whereon he encouragingly, "But "you've made your reputation in that line already." The poor fellow's life has been a saddened one ever since.

Other bags I see recorded in my note book, but none of them come up to this one of 678 lbs. by 4 rods in 3 days, and this is I trust enough to draw you with me bottom fishing. Wasn't it Artemus Ward who wrote

> "He kept a poking fun like sin
> And then a kinder rubbing on it in."

I too will do "a kinder rubbing on it in" by giving you the actual details of this bag, as recorded on the spot. How we gloated over the heaps of good fish that lay piled before us, and specially over the larger ones that represented each one of them a long hand to hand fight, the issue of which had been every instant uncertain till the very last moment, when the large landing net, several times evaded, at last engulfed and carried the still struggling captive far inland lest in unhooking he should flounder once again into the element in which he was master. How we gloated over them, and why shouldn't you too see each one as it goes to scale? The groups in which you find them recorded below are the groups in which they were piled together at a weighing in the tray of the Salter's balance. Only the finest were weighed separately. We had not time for more, and yet in England the great majority of those hastily lumped together by us would have been scrupulously weighed one by one and individually recorded in ruled columns in a neatly printed book. We also took no note of ounces. Quarters of pounds were our lowest units of weighment. A fish was either $1\frac{1}{4}$ or $1\frac{1}{2}$ lbs. according as he was over or under the intervening 2 ounces, there was not time for closer exactitude. Quick man! tip them out of the tray, and fill it up again as full as it will hold. And here is the result, copied from my rough note book made on the spot. I find that on one or two occasions some one else of the party weighed the fish, and so I got the totals from him; there are no details for those occasions.

Wednesday Morning, 8th September.

N caught	45 fish	weighing	72½	lbs.
A ,,	24 ,,	,,	27½	,,
B ,,	14 ,,	,,	7	,,
C ,,	9 ,,	,,	11½	,,
Morning Total	92 ,,	,,	118½	,,

Wednesday Evening, 8th September.

N caught	1 fish	weighing	3	lbs.
,,	2 ,,	,,	4	,,
,,	3 ,,	,,	4	,,
,,	5 ,,	,,	4½	,,
,,	6 ,,	,,	4	,,
,,	2 ,,	,,	5	,,
,,	4 ,,	,,	6	,,
,,	6 ,,	,,	6½	,,
,,	5 ,,	,,	6½	,,
,,	5 ,,	,,	4	,,
,,	8 ,,	,,	3	,,
,,	14 ,,	,,	2½	,,
N's Evening Total	61 ,,	,,	53	,,

A caught	6 fish	weighing	4½	lbs.
,,	5 ,,	,,	6	,,
,,	6 ,,	,,	5	,,
,,	12 ,,	,,	3	,,
A's Evening Total	29 ,,	,,	18½	,,

Wednesday Evening, 8th September—(continued).

B caught	1	fish weighing	4	lbs.
„	8	„ „	7	„
B's Evening Total	9	„ „	11	„
C caught	1	fish weighing	$3\frac{3}{4}$	lbs.
„	5	„ „	$5\frac{3}{4}$	„
„	10	„ „	$5\frac{1}{2}$	„
C's Evening Total	16	„ „	15	„

Thursday Morning, 9th September.

N caught	4	fish weighing	$5\frac{1}{2}$	lbs.
„	1	„ „	6	„
„	1	„ „	5	„
„	1	„ „	$4\frac{1}{2}$	„
„	5	„ „	5	„
„	7	„ „	7	„
„	9	„ „	9	„
„	7	„ „	9	„
„	9	„ „	9	„
„	8	„ „	9	„
„	10	„ „	5	„
„	20	„ „	5	„
„	11	„ „	1	„
N's Morning Total	93	„ „	80	„
A caught	35	fish weighing	$27\frac{1}{2}$	lbs.
B „	19	„ „	11	„
C „	27	„ „	17	„

Thursday Evening, 9th September.

N caught	4	fish weighing	6	lbs.
„	1	„ „	$3\frac{1}{2}$	„
„	1	„ „	$5\frac{1}{2}$	„
„	1	„ „	$4\frac{1}{2}$	„

Thursday Evening, 9*th September*—(continued).

N caught	7	fish	weighing	8	lbs.
„	7	„	„	8	„
„	10	„	„	8	„
„	11	„	„	6	„
„	16	„	„	3	„
N's Evening Total	58	„	„	52½	„
A caught	9	fish	weighing	4	lbs.
„	25	„	„	3½	„
A's Evening Total	34	„	„	7½	„
B caught	3	fish	weighing	4½	lbs.
„	5	„	„	5½	„
„	15	„	„	3½	„
B's Evening Total	23	„	„	13½	„
C caught	4	fish	weighing	5	lbs.
„	4	„	„	5	„
„	4	„	„	5½	„
„	6	„	„	6	„
„	7	„	„	5	„
„	17	„	„	5½	„
C's Evening Total	42	„	„	32	„

Friday Morning, 10*th September*.

N caught	1	fish	weighing	3½	lbs.
„	3	„	„	4	„
„	9	„	„	8	„
„	6	„	„	7	„
„	25	„	„	4½	„
N's Morning Total	44	„	„	27	„

Friday Morning, 10*th September*—(continued).

A caught	6	fish	weighing	7	lbs.
„	6	„	„	4½	„
„	23	„	„	5	„
A's Morning Total	35	„	„	16½	„

B caught	1	fish	weighing	11	lbs.
„	1	„	„	11	„
„	6	„	„	7	„
„	6	„	„	7½	„
„	19	„	„	5	„
B's Morning Total	33	„	„	41½	„

C caught	6	fish	weighing	7	lbs.
„	8	„	„	7	„
„	8	„	„	1½	„
C's Morning Total	22	„	„	15½	„

Friday Evening, 10*th September.*

N caught	9	fish	weighing	10	lbs.
„	4	„	„	6	„
„	1	„	„	4½	„
„	14	„	„	6	„
„	5	„	„	7	„
„	4	„	„	5	„
„	5	„	„	6½	„
„	5	„	„	7	„
„	8	„	„	6	„
„	6	„	„	6	„
„	8	„	„	8½	„
„	14	„	„	4	„
N's Evening Total	83	„	„	76½	„

Friday Evening, 10*th September*—(continued).

A caught	3 fish	weighing	5 lbs.
„	8 „	„	4½ „
„	20 „	„	2½ „
A's Evening Total	31 „	„	12 „

B caught	1 fish	weighing	6 lbs.
„	14 „	„	7 „
B's Evening Total	15 „	„	13 „

C caught	6 fish	weighing	7½ lbs.
„	7 „	„	7 „
„	17 „	„	4½ „
C's Evening Total	30 „	„	19 „

	N	A	B	C		Total.	
8th Morning	72½ lbs.	27½ lbs.	7 lbs.	11½ lbs.	=	118½	216 lbs.
„ Evening	53 „	18½ „	11 „	15 „	=	97½	
9th Morning	80 „	27½ „	11 „	17 „	=	135½	241 „
„ Evening	52½ „	7½ „	13½ „	32 „	=	105½	
10th Morning	27 „	16½ „	41½ „	15½ „	=	100½	221 „
„ Evening	76½ „	12 „	13 „	19 „	=	120½	
	361½ „	109½ „	97 „	110 „	=		678 „

It does not matter to the reader that A, B, C are fancy initials, but it is fair to add for his information that N was not only far and away the most practised hand at this particular style of fish, but also had the most suitable rod. B and C were comparatively new to it, C quite new, so their bags were poor indeed the first day, but improved later on. Their rods too were not what they would use now.

I hope as I said above that this tale of fish is enough to draw you with me bottom fishing? In the hope that it is I will continue.

My acquaintance with these fish has been made chiefly in ponds. I have seen them in rivers, but there I confess they have been one too many for me, but mainly I think because I gave them but secondary attention where I could get Mahseer, or was experimenting with the fly, catching Barils and Chelas, and hoping to make new discoveries.

And I am afraid it will be so to the end of my days in India that whenever I find myself by the side of a river that holds them I shall stick to my old love the mighty Mahseer. And so I am not likely to work out thoroughly the question of Labeo fishing in rivers. But I fancy it should be very similar to roach fishing where you cannot expect to do much in a river till you have got the fish together by systematic ground baiting, and constituted what is called "a swim." This I have never had the leisure to do in a river, but I suppose others have, for I am told there are places in rivers where Europeans have good sport with these fish with rods. Still my own experience has, for the reasons given, been confined to ponds, and it is from this point of view that I think this fishing is most worthy of attention.

Pond fishing has this recommendation that you can get it nearer to civilization, without the expense and organization necessary for the carriage of tents and commissariat to the banks of the forest-clad mountain river such as the Mahseer delight in. Many have not the means of making such pilgrimages. Many a poor white exile has no tents and no camp kit, and no leave to go to a distance, and yet he is still my brother angler, and I wish to show him how he too may have right royal sport fishing in India. "This is right royal sport" said one of the party that helped to kill the 678 lbs. in 3 days, from him I borrow the expression born as it was of actualities. This sport can also be had without running any risk of your servants catching fever; for catch fever they will, when Mahseer fishing, be you ever so provident for them. I have given them each a raised cot to sleep on, good tent shelter, plenty of blankets, easy marching, high feeding, boiled and filtered water for drinking, warm water for bathing, and a daily one grain of Quinine as a prophylactic, both when in camp and for 15 days after; and yet I have had them catch fever, and get pitifully ill, when every gentleman in camp escaped scot-free. Your native servants simply will not take the slightest pains to adhere to the most ordinary precautions, and of sequence pay the penalty of their provokingly childish recklessness. To say it serves them right may be true theoretically, but practically it is no remedy, and the result to myself has been that I have more than once been choked off Mahseer fishing, and had to expend my little holiday on Labeos instead. There are again other months in which you would not adventure even yourself into a Mahseer jungle, all the hot months to wit, in which you can still have Labeo fishing with perfect impunity. Indeed the hot months are the best months for them. This style of fishing has then recommendations of its own.

First I must tell you where to find it, and then how to tackle it.

Wherever you can find a pond or tank that never runs dry, and is never netted, and is fed by a freshwater channel above tidal influence from a river of which at least the higher waters are perennial, there you will assuredly find Labeos of sorts, White Carp (*Cirrhina cirrhosa*), Freshwater Sharks (*Wallago attu*) and not improbably a number of other fish of which hereafter.

I am writing primarily of the Madras Presidency, but the probabilities are of the strongest that if there are similar channel-fed tanks in the other Presidencies the like fishing may be had there, not only equally good, but in much greater perfection. In ponds in Calcutta I have seen fish that answer to ours, as for instance their Kālabous which is simply our *Labeo calbasu*, and their Rohi is only another Labeo, to wit *Labeo rohita*, and these are the very fish of which I write. Again the beautiful Mirga of Northern India is *Cirrhina mrigala*, a fish of the same genus as *Cirrhina cirrhosa*, the White Carp of which I treat, and very much like our fish, so like that a separate plate is unnecessary, only it is much finer, running to 3 ft. in length and 18 lbs. in weight. Yet again Northern India has in its ponds the Catla which is *Catla Buchanani*, a magnificent pond fish running up to 50 lbs. to my own knowledge, and I have it on excellent testimony that one of 100 lbs. weight was caught with a hook in a pond opposite the Museum on the Calcutta maidān. Burmah too has Labeos much finer than any in the Madras Presidency, one of them growing to "nearly 5 ft. in length," and in a thick fish like the Labeo this means great weight. About the Bombay side my information is less explicit, but some at least of the Labeos are to be found there, and the probabilities are that it is at least as well off as the Madras Presidency, which though in this matter it takes rank below Bengal and Burmah can still show bags such as are recorded above. The presumption then is that remarks on pond fishing in the Madras Presidency will be equally applicable in the Sister Presidencies of Bengal, Bombay and Burmah, and also in Ceylon.

The essentials of habitat are then, a tank or pond that is never dry, never netted, and is river-fed. The Southern Presidency abounds in ponds that are river-fed. I put out of consideration all the irrigation tanks, because they are ordinarily run right out every year for irrigation purposes. I refer to the innumerable tanks which are dug out for bathing and drinking purposes. Of these also a large proportion run dry in hot weather, and a still larger proportion are netted to death on contract, so netted that one would think the fishing contractor was bound down by some awful penalties not to leave a living tadpole in them. But there are still not a few which are so large and deep that they never run dry. Some of these are merely earth excavations or ponds pure and simple. Some are built up on all sides with stone steps for the convenience of bathers, and are square, each side of the square being as much as a quarter of a mile in length.

Plate IV

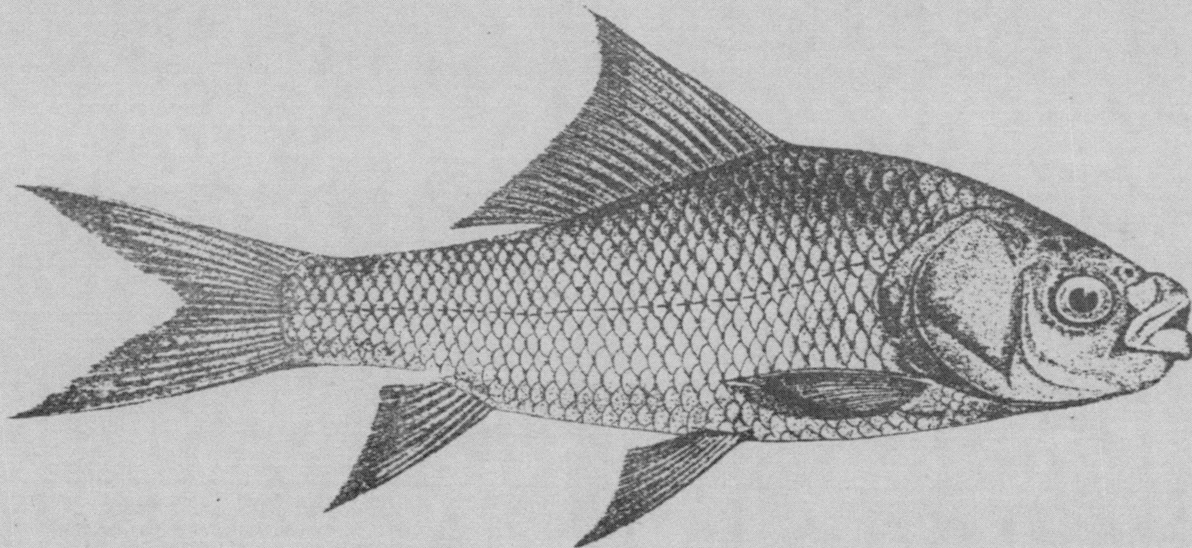

CATLA BUCHANANI

These built tanks are generally attached to a Municipality or a Temple, but are sometimes private property. In some of these all netting is strictly prohibited because a net stirs up the bottom and fouls the water, which it is desired to keep undisturbed for the benefit of the bathers and drinkers. These are the tanks you want. Whether built or not built, as long as they are not netted they are the tanks you want. The channel that feeds them may not be more than a foot wide, still if it comes from a bigger channel which comes from a perennial river it will, in flood time when the tank is filled up, bring in hosts of fry of fish of many sorts, and notably of the sorts for which we mean to fish. These fry, coming by migratory instinct down the channel, find themselves in a *cul de sac* in these ponds, and profiting by the sanatory protection abovementioned grow to 20 lbs. in weight.

Having found your pond the next thing is how to catch the fish out of it. Don't think you are going to do that as easy as shelling peas. I will confess to you that when I did not know quite as much as I do now of their tricks and their manners I have myself sat down by a tank for a whole day and taken nothing, when the very next day a splendid bag was made out of that very pond. Out of the 678 lbs. which I have mentioned above as taken by four rods in three days one rod alone took 361½ lbs. or more than half the whole bag, showing how his superior skill told, for we were all using the same bait, the same tackle, and fishing within 2 or 3 yards of each other. The other three rods took under exactly the same circumstances 109½ lbs., 110 lbs. and 97 lbs. respectively in the same time, and there was not one of the four that was not a born fisherman. This will prepare you to believe that skill of the finest order is fully called out in this fishing, though a certain friend of mine did rail at me as follows. When first we came back with the tale of our bag he was all admiration and joy even to veneration. But after a fortnight's cogitation he stole up to me at the club, and with a wicked smile upon his countenance whispered, "Thomas, I hear those were tame fish you caught, and many of them had rings in their noses!" However he is a "disciple" as he styled it, and so I can forgive him worse fibs than that.

On another occasion an Irish Doctor wanted to be laid in at this new style of fishing, so we took him and put him down between two of us, and showed him everything we could. Every bone in that Doctor's body was a poacher's from the earliest days he could toddle with a bent pin, and yet he could make nothing of it at first. He sat between two of us and saw when we struck, and saw us pulling out good fish one after another, and his own float bobbing away just as well as ours, and yet he couldn't nick them at the right second, till missing bite after bite there burst from him involuntarily "*Holy* St. Dennis," but, Saint Dennis not helping him, by and bye he gave "Holy St. Patrick" a turn, and thus working the two he got well into it at last; and now he is a happy man. And so may you be too dear reader if you are made of as good stuff, and will condescend to be painstakingly exact and smart, and perhaps you might work St. Thomas, just for a change. I don't think either of the other two know much about it. But I warn you again it is more difficult than any fishing I ever had in my life.

Now then for the tackle and mode of using it, and after these warnings you will surely neglect no detail.

Very quick striking being necessary a light rod is a *sine qua non.* Ten feet is the best length for your rod. You may perhaps have it as much as eleven feet long if you particularly wish it and it is very light, but not an inch longer be it ever so light, because the bites are so fine that you could not see them further from you. A friend prefers 11 ft. being greedy of reaching out further and getting more bites as he thinks. But I think he is the only one that does; for my own part I prefer a 10 ft. rod, both because it reaches as far out as you can see to do justice to your bites, and also because one foot off the butt end of your rod lightens it, and facilitates quicker as well as lighter striking, and adds to the pleasures of the playing of a good fish when he is on. If for this latter purpose the rod could be made lighter still, the hand to hand fight would be creamier too; but you dare not sacrifice stiffness to suppleness or you would never be able to strike quick enough. Ten feet then is the length advised for your rod.

I have done business with a light trout rod substituting a short stiff spinning top for the fly top. This shortening and stiffening quickens the stroke, but strike as quickly as you may they will still steal a great quantity of your bait. They are sons of thieves every one of them. So you had best have the very best rod you can to try and be even with them, and that is a bamboo. Not the common male bamboo, it is too heavy; nor the female bamboo, it is again too heavy. But a bamboo reed that is a beautiful compromise between the two. It is well known in Calcutta, and used by all the native fishermen for bottom fishing, and is freely exported to England and America, where it is called cane, and used for pike rods. But for pike rods too much of the fine end is cut off, and you lose all the sport of playing your fish, as well as get your rod unnecessarily heavy; and all avoidable weight is to be scrupulously barred as retarding the rapidity of your stroke. This bamboo reed of 10 ft. long is the very best rod you can possibly have, and if the tackle makers in England would so make them they would find them perfection for roach and barbel also. I have these rods because I make them up myself, and perhaps you can do the same. If not Messrs. Oakes & Co., Madras are, at my instance, getting the bamboo reeds from Calcutta and making them up; and doubtless other tackle shops will take to doing the same when this kind of angling is understood. I will therefore be a little more explicit about the making of them up. Suppose we name them Labeo Rods that they may have a specific name by which anglers may know how to order them, and tackle makers know how to advertise them.

Labeo rods are made then out of bamboo reeds which are supplied from the forests in the neighbourhood of Calcutta, and the probability is that the same reed grows in the Madras and Bombay Presidencies also, but unfortunately it is not known to natives as an article of trade, and we cannot therefore get it except from Calcutta. Those sent me by favor of a friend were cut in 17 or 18 feet lengths, tapering from an inch in diameter at the base to $\frac{1}{8}$th of an inch in diameter at the tip. They are not straight when cut, but by means of oil and fire and pressure applied when green, which the natives there thoroughly understand, they are supplied as straight as an arrow from end to end. They are not all exactly uniform in thickness, some being slightly more hollow than others, so that there would seem to be more sorts than one. The lightest and the most tapering are the ones I prefer. Measuring 10 ft. from the fine end, saw off the rest with a fine cross-grain saw. Take it in your hand, it is quite a different thing from what you thought it was when you felt it in the long 18 ft. piece. But it is small to grip in the hand for any length of time, so saw off 16 inches of the thick end which you have discarded, saw it so that you shall have one of the natural joints in the bamboo quite at one end so as to make a solid butt. From the other end of the 16 inches it will be hollow. Put the butt end of the first cut thin rod into this hollow, and it will make the best handle you can wish. In putting it in it may not always fit, either it has to be shaved down slightly, or it has to be enlarged by whipping a good stout cord round it. Having made it fit, so that you can push the thin butt into the hollow butt right home to the bamboo joint in the hollow butt, make a pencil mark, so that you may know when it is home, and taking it out, smear the thin butt end with warm marine glue, and put it in again, and push it right home up to the pencil mark. The marine glue should be enough to make every part of the thin butt hold to the hollow butt all the way up, so that the two may be one piece in the hand and never vibrate. This is a much better handle than any made of wood. It is large enough to give a comfortable grip to the hand, it is of uniform lightness with the rest of the rod, and it is stronger than any wood.

My lightest trout fly-rod the "duck" weighs 10 ounces without the winch, one pound with it. My Labeo rods weigh 8 and 9 ounces without the winch.

Put on the winch, a small one of 2¼ inches in diameter, close down to the end of the butt.

Put on the eye at the end of the rod as usual and *small* standing rings. There is no sense in putting them on of varying sizes enlarging towards the butt. It is an old world idea. Use the *smallest* standing rings you can get, and have them *all* of the smallest size from tip to winch.

If it be possible never cut the rod. It plays so much better in one piece. Carry it about in a female bamboo, split down lengthwise so as to open into two pieces. Knock out the joints, and one or two rods will lie neatly in this light but strong case. Lash it round in three or four places, and the rods inside are perfectly secure. By rail lash it to the iron supports of the foot-board of your carriage and it will be in nobody's way, and safe, and under your eye.

When at home never lean it in a corner, or it will get a permanent bend in it, nor lay it on the ground or it will get trodden on and split. For though these rods are exceedingly strong in playing a fish they won't stand a blow, but easily split. Keep them hung in your sanctum sanctorum as a whipmaker does his whips, suspended by a whip cord and button, with a single hitch from one nail.

If you must cut these rods for portability I thought the best way to retain their lightness was by one splice. But I find a bamboo won't stand splicing, it becomes weak at that point, and gives under the strain of a heavy fish, even though you take the precaution of making the splice a long six-inch one, and fill in the hollow with well fitting bamboo or wood glued in. A ferrule is the only thing. But of course you will only cut your bamboo into two pieces, not three, and have the butt piece a full inch or more longer than the thin end, so as to protect it in carriage.

For the first month or two after cutting examine from time to time to see that the bamboos are not attacked by bamboo borers. If you detect one stop him up with copal varnish, a mere touch on his bore is enough. He won't try it again.

If you cannot get a rod of this sort then I would say order a roach rod from England; or shorten and stiffen your trout rod as above suggested. If it brings it down to less than 10 ft. it is better for quick striking than having your rod too long.

A word, in passing, on why I have insisted on a stiff rod, instead of a pliable, as essential to quick striking. A pliable rod, your trout fly-rod for instance, does not give effect to your upward stroke till the tip has first struck downwards, and recovering from this, has sprung back in the direction in which you originally struck. Try it. Sit close down to the water, holding your hand and rod point both as close to the water as you can without actually touching it. In this position strike upwards smartly as if you were striking for a fish. You will find that the point of your fly-rod instead of striking upwards in the same direction as the stroke of your hand, will first strike downwards and hit the water, and not till it has recovered itself from this first downward motion will it strike upwards, and impart to the line and fish the stroke which you wished to deliver. The time then between your stroke, and the pliable fly-rod recovering from its first opposite motion, and delivering your stroke to the fish, is lost in a pliable rod. And the loss is fatal to quick striking, the very quick striking necessary for Labeos.

Try again another way. Lay your pliable fly-rod on the

table, and place a rupee on the table just touching the point of the rod, and on its left. Then try and strike to the right parallel with the plane of the table, that is to say strike away from the rupee. You would expect that the rod point would answer your strike, and spring to the right. On the contrary the rupee will first be sent flying, and afterwards the rod point will recover itself and repeat your strike to the right.

Theoretically the same thing occurs more or less with every rod that is not absolutely rigid, but it is so much minimized in a stiff rod that, for all practical purposes, the objection is got rid of.

A reel and running line you will need of course, thirty yards of the latter is ample; and it is as well to have both as light as may be, though these are the parts of your tackle about which you need be least particular. Still for running line my preference is for thin tussa-silk line, it is so light, so strong and so elastic. You can get it of Oakes & Co., Popham's Broadway, Madras; of D. N. Biswas & Co., 32, Dalhousie Square, Calcutta; and doubtless also of R. B. Rodda & Co., 7 & 8, Dalhousie Square, Calcutta; and of Manton & Co., 13, Old Court House Street, Calcutta; and of J. P. Luscombe & Co., Old Ice House, 29, Elgin Road, Allahabad. You are ordinarily recommended to take the twist and fear of kinking out of your tussa-silk line by suspending a brick bat from an upper storey, and letting it unravel itself. But what I prefer is this, taken from *The Badminton Library:*

Recipe for Waterproofing.—Mix cold copal varnish and gold size in the proportion of ten parts of the former to one part of the latter. Soak the line in this dressing for a couple of days or more if you like, the jar in which it is placed being air tight. Then stretch the line to dry. The line will not be fit for use for three or four weeks of hot summer weather in England, and no rain or dew must be allowed to come to it while drying. But 3 or 4 days of hot-weather tropical sun will dry it through and through in India.

I put the coil into the mixture just as it is received from the shop, and when thoroughly soaked stretch it out just as it is, carefully avoiding untwisting it by attempting to take out any kinks. I simply stretch it in one long line from tree to tree. Every kink will disappear without any untwisting, and when the dressing has dried and hardened, it will be found that the line is stiff and wire-like, with all its twist preserved, and yet with no tendency to spring into a kink on being slack.

At the end of this I use just two lengths of single salmon gut, no more is necessary, and the hook on another length of the same. Even these two extra lengths of gut may be dispensed with if you like, and the thin tussa-silk line tied direct to the length of gut on which the hook is, for the fish's eye is set downwards, and they seem to look chiefly down at the bottom and not up at your line. Try drawn gut, or even stout trout gut, if you like, but you will soon give it up, for you will find that it is practically impossible to strike as quick as you must for these fish, and as hard as is necessary to drive the hook into their leathery mouths, without using more violence than drawn gut or even stout trout gut will stand. The mouths of these fish are much tougher than those of roach, and the hook used is a much larger one, therefore the stroke necessary to drive the hook in past the barb has, on both grounds, to be much harder than a roach fisher would endorse.

The absolute necessity for striking instantly at the very right second tends to leading one into striking unnecessarily hard, and not a few times have I seen even salmon gut snapped at the strike. But that is not right. That is not the fault of the gut but of the striker. Let me warn you not to follow herein the example of the gentleman, don't say he is a mythological personage, who got insensibly striking smarter and smarter, till one day his friends began to doubt if he was quite as light handed as he might be when they found a 30 lb. fish up in a tree behind him!

You have then to strike very quickly, as quickly indeed as possible at the critical second, and with a certain amount of strength, say with strength enough to snap drawn gut, and even good strong medium trout gut, but not to break salmon gut, and yet not with violence.

In order to be able to see the critical second for striking your float must be most sensitive. A porcupine quill is all too coarse an implement. The natives use a 4 to 6 inch piece of the stalk of a large grass, and laying the running line on it whip a little cotton round both, close up to one end of the float. The float is thus attached to the line, and the line will, with a little persuasion, run up and down under the whipping if you wish to alter your depth, but the friction is enough to keep it from doing so of itself. At least the friction of the whipping is supposed to be enough for this purpose, but I have found it sometimes fail me after the float and line have become sodden from being some time in the water, and little by little the depth alters, which is fatal to good fishing, for as we shall see hereafter the depth must be exact. I have therefore slightly modified the native float. I take a long tail feather of a peacock, and cut off the quill part, till we get to the solid pithy opaque white stem. The part of this stem which is nearest the bird is a trifle thicker than the rest which tapers gradually. I used at one time to use the thicker end as well as the rest, and that poaching son of Holy St. Dennis does so still and prefers a 5 inch length of it, but after very close comparison of wary bites I am convinced he is wrong, and that it is not by any means an immaterial point that I can leave to the angler's fancy. I am convinced that in wary biting the thicker stem will not be as sensitive and as indicative as the thinner. I therefore cut off and throw away as much of the stem as is more than $\frac{2\frac{1}{2}}{16}$ths of an inch in width, and then I cut the rest in 6 inch lengths till the stem gets to less than $\frac{2}{16}$ths of an inch in width, when it becomes too thin and frail to stand much use.

The stem of the peacock's quill is not round but slightly oval, and the above measurements are taken across the broadest part of the oval. It is easily done with a compass or gauge screwed to the right gape. The thicker part of the quill is only $\frac{1}{16}$th or $\frac{1\frac{1}{2}}{16}$th of an inch thicker, and you may think I am mighty particular. I am, but intentionally, because I think it will add to your sport. One of the peacock tail-feather quills is 4 or 5 ft. long, and you will only get 2 or 3 of my 6 inch floats out of it, whereas you might cut 6 or 7 out of one quill if you are not particular. But the quills are not expensive. You may get a bundle of 18 or 20 for 4 annas.

Remove the harl, not by stripping, as it tears off the shiny skin of the stem, but by neatly snipping. The float will not then get so readily sodden in the water.

Then to one end, the thinner end for preference, a small loop of thick salmon running line is whipped on so as to project a quarter of an inch by outside measurement, and dipped in varnish to stiffen it. I tried a wire loop first but I found it cut the line. This loop or eye is for attaching your float to your line, and it forms the bottom end of the float as it stands in the water. Then we commence work on the top of the float. The surface of the very end where it has been cut is left white to attract the eye, but all round the float for half an inch down is painted bright vermillion in oil color. Then half an inch of float is left the natural white, and the third half-inch painted again a band of bright vermillion. Then there is another half-inch band left white, and the next half-inch band is painted vermillion, and the rest of the float is left its natural white. Thus we have the very tip white, followed by alternate half-inch bands of vermillion and white, till we have three vermillion bands, which is enough, as the float rides in the water with most of the white unbanded part submerged.

The object of the alternate red and white bands is to aid your eye in detecting such slight depressions of the float as would otherwise be imperceptible, and you will find occasions when the little white tip will prove invaluable. But you will understand these difficulties when we come to discussing the manner of biting. For the present we are getting the tackle ready.

In the Frontispiece there is a break in the float because my page will not allow me to make it the full 6 inches.

You will observe that in the drawing, Plate I, the float is represented as riding with a slight tilt on it, and not perfectly upright. The reason for this is that in that position the slightest tension from the fish sucking at your bait makes the float stand upright, which is a larger movement than a slight depression, and catches your eye more quickly. Of the fishermen that I have seen at this work the most successful N, prefers this tilt, but some on the other hand prefer an upright float. You are graciously permitted to do as you like, now that I have duly warned you of the advantage gained by the tilt. Still I only recommend a slight tilt as in the diagram. The thing may be overdone.

You will see again that this float, which I will call The Detective, differs from the English floats ordinarily used for roach in having the line attached to one end only. The upper end is thus left perfectly free, and is consequently much more sensitive than if it was weighted with a heavy sodden piece of running line dangling from it into the water; and when you gather up your line in preparedness for a strike you do not affect the float so much as if the line was fastened at the top also. In short there is no rhyme or reason in fastening the line to both ends of the float, one end is quite enough to prevent your losing your float, and for detective purposes much better.

And then why do I use a loop instead of the simpler English sliding cap. Because the loop is at the very end of the float, whereas a cap necessarily slips up more or less till it bites tight, and in the former case you get the indication of the bite magnified by the leverage of the length of the float, a leverage which is again increased by having the float 6 inches long in preference to 5. This may seem a very trifle, but wait till you have seen the bites for yourself. Wait till you have sat as I have for a whole day watching a float and complaining that nothing but minnows or the like were biting, little bits of wretches that were only made for the purpose of stealing your bait and were not worth catching, wait till you have done this and in consequence caught nothing, whereas you might have caught a cooly load or two of fish running from 1 to 6 or 7 lbs. and more, wait till you have done this, and see if you do not agree with me that no pains should be spared in making your float as sensitive as possible for the detection of these sons of thieves, Labeos, and White Carp.

I have then a loop of varnished salmon running-line at the bottom of the float, and the way in which the float is put on is simplicity itself. Double the running line at about the place where you wish to have your float, pass the doubled end through the loop or eye at the end of the float, and drawing enough through, pass the loop thus formed in the running line over the float, and bring it down, and pull it as shewn in the diagram. It will never slip in the least.

If you want to change your depth the knot must be loosened and the upper or lower end pulled according as you wish your length below the float less or more.

This loosening of the knot is considered troublesome by some, and it is also objected that in picking open the knot, which gets very tight from striking and playing big fish, the running line is liable to get frayed and weakened at that point. There may be something in the objection, but there is not much to my thinking, and I prefer this simple knot on the whole for the main reason that it never slips, and once having got my depth with the greatest exactitude to my complete satisfaction I know I can keep it without the slightest alteration all the day, or for a week for that matter, unless I get a hook or line carried away earlier. But *quot homines tot sententiæ*, and some consider the slackening and shifting of the knot a nuisance. For them I substitute the alternative plan also shewn in the diagram. It is this :—

Make a quill cap which shall fit the float tight close down to the loop end. The cap must be whipped round to prevent its splitting when forced on tightly. Before knotting your running line on to your hook gut, pass the running line through the eye of the float and through the cap, and push the cap into position on the float, pushing it from the loop end upwards, not from the top end downwards as in an English float. Then tie your hook gut to the running line, put on your sinker, and proceed to find the depth at which to fish. For the temporary purpose of finding the bottom the cap is easily slipped off and on at the lower end of the float, and bites enough to prevent shifting then. But when you have your depth to a nicety, and want to be assured of no change taking place from slipping, I don't think the bite of the cap is quite assurance enough, and I add to it the following simple precaution, shewn in the diagram :—Slip the cap down and off the float at the lower or loop end, taking care that in doing it the line does not shift in the slightest degree, and holding the loop or eye in the float so that the lower or hook end of the line shall not shift, pass the upper or rod end of the running line three times round the outside of the float loop, as if you were whipping or binding it, then lay it on the float and pass the cap over it. It cannot shift in the least.

You will please observe that in this plan, as well as in the previous one without a cap, the principle is carefully preserved of keeping one only point of attachment of the line to the float close down to the lower end, the upper end being quite free, and that the point of connection with the fish's bite is the extreme lowest end, so that you may have the advantage of preserving all the leverage the six-inch float can give you in indicating the bites. On no account let the cap come any way up the float, or you weight the top with the line, and interfere with its freedom and indicativeness.

There is one little objection to this latter method. The float is made of frail material, and will not bear much pushing on and off of the cap, and unless very carefully handled is prone to double up when sodden. But in no case can such very light material be very durable, and such floats can never be very expensive to make. I keep them ready by the dozen but then it is true I have to do the same with all tackle, as my friends, long may they do it, have a way of using my tackle and breaking and losing it for me at a grand rate. "It is well I have a good supply" I said one day rejoicingly, as fish were carrying away hook after hook, and now and then a float. "Yes it is" said my cheery friend, as he helped himself again out of my box, "it would never do for *you* to run short."

It is therefore an open question which of the two styles of float you use, a matter of personal preference. I think tackle shops should always make them with the cap, and the angler should always buy them thus, for then he always leaves himself the option of throwing away the cap and using the loop only, if he finds he prefers it.

Now for the hook. I think an eyed Limerick is the best for this fishing. I prefer eyed hooks whenever I can use them because hooks draw so terribly in India, that you can never trust a whipped hook a second season, even though you have bound it yourself, and know it is thoroughly well done. I have heard tackle-shops complained of because of their cheaply tied hooks, whereas it was not the tieing that was really to blame, but the climate. If you are fishing with a worm you must have whipped hooks because the eye presents an obstacle that you cannot pass the worm over. But for a paste bait and for a fly the eye is no objection, while it has this great advantage that it cannot draw, and you can and should tie the gut on fresh just before fishing, so that you may know it is not rust eaten, but is thoroughly trustworthy.

Eyed hooks are made in different ways, with the metal eye flat with the shank, or say at right angles when the hook is lying on its side on the table, this is called needle eyed; with the eye inclined towards the barb, which is called turned down; with the eye inclined away from the barb, which is known as turned up. Their respective advantages are discussed at length in *The Badminton Library*. Without bringing the controversy into these limited pages I will simply say that whichever hook you have you must accommodate your tieing to it so as to make the point of tension on the line lie parallel with the point of the hook.

If the hook is needle eyed pass the gut through from either side of the eye, and without going round the shank pass it through the same way a second time, and then tie a common single knot with the short end round the long end of the gut, and pulling it tight work it close up to the metal eye, and snip off the end.

If the metal eye is turned down, first insert the end of your gut on the upper side of the eye, that is the side furthest away from the barb, and passing it once half round the shank, put it again through the eye from the lower side, so that both ends of gut come out at the upper side of the eye, then with the short end of gut tie a single knot round the long end of gut, pull tight, work up close, and snip off the end as before.

If the metal eye is turned up commence by inserting your end of gut from the lower side, and proceed as in the former knot, the result being that both ends of gut will in this case come out at the lower side of the eye, that is the side nearest the barb.

In all these three knots the snipped off end of gut will lie parallel with, and pointing in the same direction as, the long end of gut.

There are other ways of knotting on a hook, but these are enough for our fishing, and my aim now is not so much to be exhaustive as to produce a cheap little volume which shall be within the means of every Indian angler; for this reason I do not give plates of knots, though I dare say I may do it if ever I bring out a third edition of *The Rod in India*, with this matter included. Meanwhile all my aim is unpretentiously, and as economically as possible, to aid every brother of the angle, be his means ever so small, and his family ever so large, still to enjoy this the cheapest and most accessible of all fishing, tank fishing.

The next point is the size of the hook. I commenced fishing for these fish with a No. 6 Kirby or Sneck bend. But gradually we have gone on enlarging our hooks till most of us have come to prefer No. 1 Limerick. One holds his hand at No. 3 and will go no larger. I quote from the sizes given in Plate III in *The Rod in India.* We also tried a treble hook, and one small hook tied immediately above another; but eventually concluded that we could not improve on a No. 1 Limerick.

For some time we fished without weighting the line at all, relying on the weight of the paste bait, a lump at least as big as your thumb nail, or bigger as sufficient. Your float being the sensitive one we have made it, such a lump of bait sufficed to pull it under if the bait was off the bottom, and to give it a tilted or upright position if the bait was just touching the bottom, while if your bait was stolen the float immediately told you of it by lying down flat. If you are not pestered with little fish then it is better not to use any weight at all. But we found that all sorts of small carps

Plate V

SCALE OF LIMERICK HOOKS

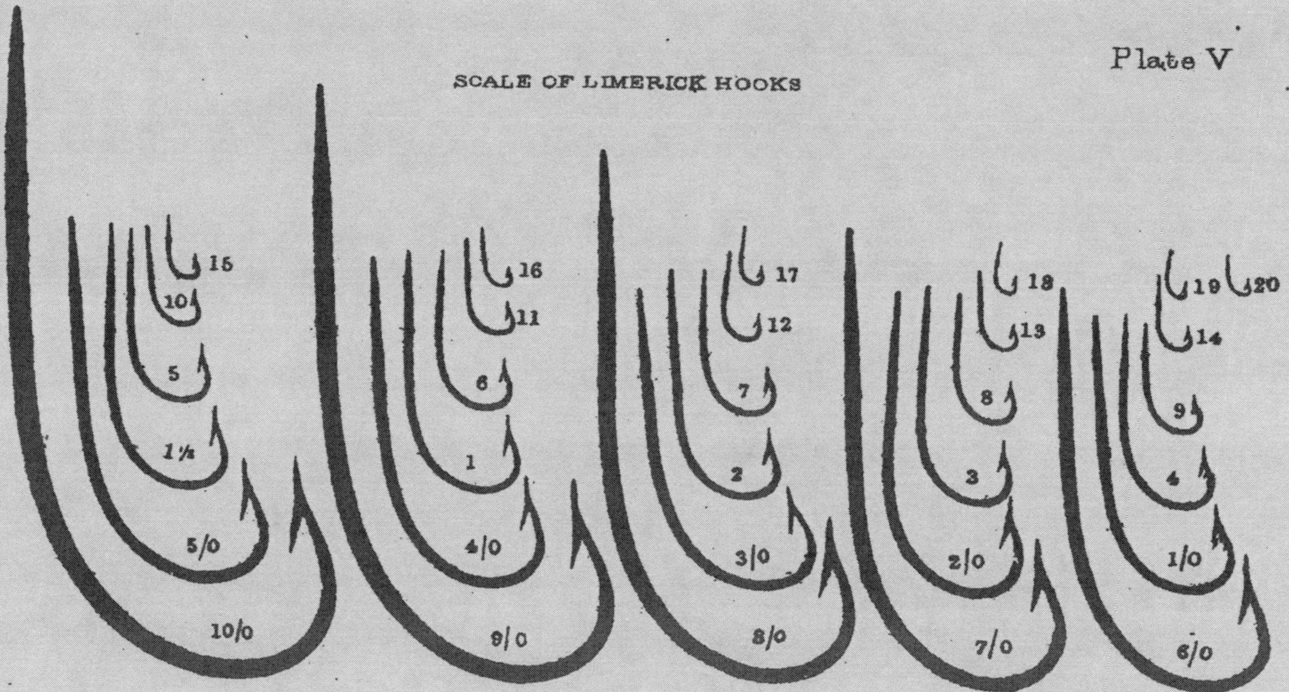

about two inches long, minnows, chelas, and such like, came round us in swarms, and, as the bait was slow in sinking, they just had a fine lively game of foot-ball with it, and knocked it all to pieces before it got to the bottom; and as it is off the bottom that the big fish feed, and on the bottom that your bait must lie, we didn't see the same fun in the foot-ball antics as the little fish did. It was necessary therefore to apply a weight for the sole purpose of making your bait sink quickly. Yet to apply it, as the ordinary Englishman does, by shot pinched on to the line, would be to leave you always uncertain as to whether your bait was actually tipping the bottom as it should be, and to destroy the sensitiveness of the float altogether; for it will be obvious that if the tilt, or upright position of the float, depended on the shot on the line, and was independent of the bait, your bait might be lying on the ground with an inch or two of slack line between it and the float, and then of course the directness of your communication would be lost, and your bait easily abstracted by these sons of thieves, without your float giving you any indication of it. So we, being anything but ordinary Englishmen, devised the following:—Take some soft lead wire, as made by the Manchester Cotton Twine Spinning Company, pass it through the eye of the Limerick hook, and bring it down the back or outside of the shank, the side away from the barb, to a little short of level with the point of the barb, and then twist the longer end of the lead wire round both the shank and this short end of lead wire again and again till you come nearly down to level with the barb, and then nip it off with the thumb nail. You then have the weight disposed on the hook itself, so that it aids instead of obstructing the exact indication of when the bait is on the bottom. It is also disposed as much as possible out of the way of the barb, and the strike. You must be careful of this or it will have the effect of narrowing the gape of the hook, and robbing you of all the advantages of a large hook. The object of passing the lead wire through the eye of the hook and bringing it a little way down the back of the shank is twofold. Firstly it prevents the lead wire slipping down the shank of the hook, and resting in the bend of the hook, which it certainly will, to the injury both of strike and hook hold, if you do not take this little precaution. Secondly the metal eye is sometimes made a little incompletely, so that the gut can slip out. The lead stops the gap against this. Now look at the plate on the Frontispiece and you will see that the bait covers all this arrangement of lead, and the end, rapid sinkage, is attained without injuring the detective powers of the float.

Well now you have got rod, and line, and float, and hook, and the next thing you want is the bait. We experimented on a great many before we arrived at the following :—

Recipe for Bait.—Boil rice, having drained and steamed it dry as for the table, mash it up quite fine on a curry-stone. Of this take two parts. Roast ground-nuts as you would coffee berries. It brings out their smell. Then grind them into fine powder. Of this take one part. Roast and grind coriander in the same way, and take one quarter part. Mix these thoroughly, kneading them well together till of one uniform consistency and color.

To aid you in procuring the materials I may as well tell you that ground-nut (*Arachis Hypogœa* Linn :) is in

Hindustani.—*Vilāyeti-mūng.*
Tamil.—*Vērk-kădălai*, or *Nilak-kădălai.*
Telugu.—*Vēru shanaga*, or *Vērushanaga-kāya.*
Malayàlim.—*Nelak-katalā*, or *Vērk-katala.*
Canarese.—*Nelagale-kāyi.*
Bengàli.—*Chīnā-bādām*, or *Bilāti-mung.*
Mahratti.—*Bhōī-chanē.*
Guzratti.—*Bhōya-chenā.*
Cingalese.—*Rata-caju.*
Burmese.—*Mībē.*

Coriander (*Coriandrum sativum* Linn:) is in

Arabic.—*Kuzbarah.*
Persian.—*Kashnīz.*
Hindustani.—*Dhanyā.*
Dukhni.—*Dhanyan.*
Tamil.—*Kottamalli.*
Telugu.—*Daniyālu*, or *Kotimiri.*
Malyālim.—*Kottam-pālari*, or *Kotta-malli.*
Canarese.—*Kottamari-bījā.*
Bengāli.—*Dhanya-ā.*
Sanscrit.—*Kustumbaru*, or *Dhānyākam.*
Mahratti.—*Dhana.*
Guzratti.—*Dhāna.*
Cingalese.—*Dhanalu*, or *Kottamalli-atta.*
Burmese.—*Nana-zi.*

Fish are attracted not a little by scent, and the roasted coriander is for this purpose. I expect it raises in their minds visions of a fine curry in preparation. The roasted ground-nut is also primarily for imparting an attractive scent to your bait, but it also answers the purpose of giving it a proper consistency. The rice alone is too sloppy, and would tumble off your hook in no time. The ground-nut taken alone is too friable, and would equally tumble off from that reason. The two mixed in the proportions given form a bait of a good tough consistency. If in roughly guessing the proportions by eye you find you have not quite hit it off, and your bait is a trifle too sloppy or too friable, you can rectify it by adding a little more either of the ground-nut or of the rice. At one time we used to neutralise the sloppiness of the rice by adding a little bran; but the bran is more easily overdone than the ground-nut, and it adds no scent to speak of. Therefore you had better make up your toughness in the bait by the addition of ground-nut; though it will do you no harm to remember that bran also may be used for this purpose when you cannot get ground-nut, or can be used sparingly even when you can get ground-nut.

If there are two or three of you fishing together you will want a lump nearly the size of your head for a day's use, for the sons of thieves will steal a great lot of it, and it will employ the whole time of an attendant to mix your bait, roll it up in balls of the required size, and always keep you well supplied with a number at your side ready for putting on quickly. He will of course quit his work for the landing net whenever you have a fish on.

You will do well to use ground bait till you have collected the fish about you. The simplest is bran, any bran, not necessarily wheaten. Do not throw it in dry, or it will blow away from you, and float away from you, and do you more harm than good. Thoroughly soak it, that is all, and it will sink quite fast enough. No clay or anything else is needed. Keep throwing in a handful from time to time, but always just on the shore side of your float, so that the fish have to come past your bait to get to it. Simple bran clouds the water, and attracts the fish without in any way satisfying them.

Other baits and ground baits there are which I will give you later on. The Index will guide you to them. But just now I see you are in a hurry to get to the actual fishing, and we have got enough for the present, so we will proceed to the water's side.

Select for your fishing a place where the bottom is as level as you can get it, and find this out by plumbing. Take the depth with a plummet on your hook exactly under the point of your rod, because that is the extreme distance at which your float ought to be for you to be able to see the bites, and because it is the position in which you can strike most effectively. Having put your float to the right depth, and tried it again to satisfy yourself, try a foot or more all round the selected spot that you may know that there is no variation of depth. You can't be too careful about getting the depth exactly, and trimming your float to it to a fraction of an inch. Note exactly where you sit so that after getting up to play and land a good one you may return to the very same place and you will do well to be very exact about it, for it is remarkable how very local the fish become when congregated at the place you have ground baited and where your bait, lost at every stroke, falls. Don't you fidget about looking for the fish, but stick to the same place, the fish will come to you; for you have attracted the attention of their visual organs by giving the water a clouded milky appearance with bran, and you have appealed also to their sense of smell, which is very keen in fishes, by the odours of the roasted coriander and roasted ground-nut. First of all little fish of sorts will swarm round you. You may think them a nuisance, but they are a good sign in their way, they are the skirmishers, and as soon as the big fish see them busy, they take the hint, and come and have a look in for themselves, just to see what is up. The big fish very soon drive the little fish off if they want the bait. I have again and again had a bite the moment my float was in, which I could see from its manner was from one of these wretched little urchins, but very soon the bite stopped for a second, and was followed by quite a different, much more cautious sort of bite, which one welcomed immediately as that of a Labeo, and in due course the strike was followed by the satisfactory sense of being well taut into something heavy and dogged, that was going to dispute every inch of line with you.

When the Labeo have found you out, they will sometimes come up and roll about on the surface all round you. When they do this it is a first class sign that they are on the move, and in taking mood. Yet it is on the bottom that you will take them, and not near the surface, so do not alter your depth, though you see them come up to the surface. They seem to come up only in sport, and to go down to the bottom for business. You may also see them basking at the top with their mouths open, and seemingly taking in the scum. But we never caught them on the surface, though we have tried them again and again. Our practical experience is that the place to take them is off the bottom, and that is why such stress is laid on your having your bait resting actually on the bottom.

If you examine the mouth of the first Labeo you catch you will find in its peculiar formation strong confirmatory reason for fishing on the bottom. The mouth is not in front as in a trout dace or roach, but it is well underneath, the snout protruding some way beyond it. It is also fimbriated, or surrounded with quite a frill of short tentacles, with which it would seem to finger its food. There is no mouth cavity as in an ordinary fish, but the tough muscular lips end abruptly in a constricted throat. Thus it would seem that it is most convenient to them to get well over their food, and to finger it into the mouth with these short tentacles, and compress it between the lips before swallowing; and we conjecture that this it is that accounts for their peculiar way of biting. I could wish I had some in an aquarium so as to study their mode of feeding, and make sure that this conjecture, based on the formation of the mouth and the conduct of the float corresponding thereto, is right. We might thus reduce conjecture to certainty. But the hundredweights of fish caught on the basis of this conjecture would seem sufficient argument that, for an angler's purposes, it is not very far wrong.

With the White Carp also the same is the case, though perhaps not quite so markedly. The mouth orifice is placed well below the protruding snout, and the mouth cavity is small.

Well then as there is not a large mouth cavity you do not expect to see the bait taken in at once. When therefore you see a few bold bobs quickly followed by the float going suddenly under and running right off quickly, any one can

Plate VI

BARBUS CHRYSOPOMA

tell that that means that some fish has taken the bait well into its mouth, and is moving away with it in the process of swallowing it, and that of course that is your time for striking. That is the style of biting you expect from a fish with an ordinary mouth. But that is not the sort of bite you will get from a Labeo. It is the bite of an Olive Carp which has an ordinary mouth orifice placed in front and an ordinary mouth cavity. Still as this fish is usually found in the same water with Labeo and White Carp it is not difficult to fail to observe that it is the Olive Carp and not the White Carp or Labeo that bite in this fashion, and there is the consequent probability that, embued with English ideas on the subject of biting, you may be expecting such bites and waiting for them and so losing the opportunity of striking when you should for the less obvious Labeo and White Carp bites. Hence it is well to eliminate these bites. Of course you will strike for them when you get them and they are simple and easy. But you will bear in mind that they are not the bites you are expecting from the better fish.

Labeo bites vary much with the circumstances, and the following are some of the styles of bite you must look out for as the ordinary ones, often varying in the course of a single day with the state of the weather or with the size of the fish.

Sometimes the float will move *slowly* up and down a few times; there's no manner of use in striking then, even though the float goes almost under, but when this is followed by a quick succession of rapid short jerky up and down twitches, strike instantly; for you won't have many of them. Within three or four of them your bait will be gone. You must therefore be looking out for them from the moment you see your float moving at all, and have your slack line cautiously gathered up, and the rod point straight over your float, and all in intensest preparedness for an instantaneous, yes instantaneous strike the moment you see the more vigorous and rapid jerky style of bobbing commence. It is a rapid up and down twitch of $\frac{1}{8}$th or $\frac{1}{16}$th of an inch in depth rather than what is commonly considered a bob. This is beautiful *bold* biting, when they are biting at their best; and when you have struck and got nothing, you feel in your innermost soul that you ought never to have missed such a bite. Still you do times without number. Why? I think because the short rapid movement means that while up to that point the Labeo had been fumbling the bait into its mouth, it is then chumping or compressing it between its lips, so as to reduce it to a size that can go down its small throat. With a soft material like a paste bait this chumping is effected very rapidly, and in a second or at most two seconds your bait is in pieces and the hook left. The critical time for striking, the time when the bait is actually between the fish's lips, is then exceedingly short-lived, and knowing this you are apt from over-excitement to strike sometimes just a little too soon; but very far oftener you are not *quick* enough, the chumping has begun and is over before you can take advantage of it. Your strike must be executed within the second during which the three or four twitches are seen. If it follows them by ever so short an interval you are too late. The bite is over and you have so to speak fired behind your bird. Nothing but practice will give you the necessary promptitude. The first few fumbling bobs are your warning, and the response within you should be, thank you, I'm ready, ready at a moment's notice to strike with unhesitating decision the very very second you commence real business with those short jerky twitches of yours, but not before. Your mind must be fully made up, and you must learn, practice only can teach you, to distinguish with certainty between the fumbling slow bobs which are preparatory, and the quick jerky twitches which supervene, and which are to be taken instant advantage of with such prompt decision.

But there is yet another difficulty and this to my mind is the greatest of all. Ah me! What anguish I have gone through with it. It has taken months off my life. But the survival of and triumph over it has put them on again, so all's well that ends well; and now my anxiety is that you may be saved from like agony of mind; and you may, in a measure, not altogether, but still in some measure, if only you will trust your *fidus Achates*, and swear by St. Thomas instead of "*Holy* St. Dennis" or even "San Path-rick." It is this. Again and again you will strike at the right time, *seemingly*, and yet not get your fish, and the result will be that you will lose confidence in yourself, and vary your stroke. It is fatal. Don't do it. Stick to it, you struck quite rightly that time; and yet you didn't get him! Why not? Because they're sons of thieves. That's it, they're sons of thieves every one of them. If the Police caught every thief, thieving wouldn't pay, and the Police would soon find their occupation gone. And so with you, if after having the whole law of striking lucidly laid down for you, and a detective float provided, you struck every Labeo that bit, not only would Labeo cease to exist, but there would be no fun in it. It is the extreme difficulty of this fishing that constitutes its chief attraction. And having overcome the difficulties by the exercise of closely critical observation, intense preparedness, and the very promptest decision of character, combined with keen eye-sight, and a quick hand, you are rewarded with tangible weight, such as I have told you of, and a very game fighting fish. Therefore I beg of you don't lose confidence in yourself, but strike, and continue to strike, just as I have told you, till you confirm your confidence by captures.

But the above I have warned you refers to *bold* biting, the easiest biting. When the fish are biting more charily, the premonitory obvious bobs dwindle down to such a slight up and down movement of the float, that you might not observe it, if it were not for the aid afforded to the eye by the alternate rings of white and red on the detective float; and the rapid succession of jerky twitches, on which you are to rely for giving you the right second at which to strike, minimized microscopically to little more than a tremor, a quiver, a shiver, a vibration. Still the principle that underlies both is the same, it is *rapidity* of movement, quick succession of short movement that is to be your guide.

Sometimes it comes to this, aye and not at all unfrequently, that there are no premonitory bobs, there is simply a slight depression of the float, so slight that it is with difficulty perceived, and it is only the slight lessening of the tilt in the direction of the horizontal position, or the nearing of the lowest red band on the float to the water level that enables you to detect it. There is this slight depression, and then the float is stationary, the depression *continuing* or still better increasing. If the depression, be it ever so slight, *continues*, look out, there's a first class pickpocket at work, and the moment you see a hardly perceptible tremor, strike. You are safe of a good one. The *principle* you will see is the same as in the bold biting, and it is simply the bold biting microscopically reduced, the quick succession of rapid short jerky bobs being minimized into a rapid tremor. Rapidity of movement in the float is the guide as to when you are to strike.

Sometimes again there is not only a slight depression in the float, but it goes almost under or even right under. If the descent of the float is *slow* don't strike, there is no use in it; but if it is pretty quick, and it goes right under and out of sight, you may strike. I don't say you will get him but you should risk it, and the odds are it will be an Olive Carp though Labeo have been taken thus occasionally.

I will illustrate this principle by a case in point. Down went the float slowly, slowly, till it was quite under water, and I could just see the white top close below the surface, and there it was stationary, and eyes were being strained to the utmost, till there came a slight tremor over the just perceptible white tip. Instantly I struck, and was into and duly landed a seven pounder.

This gives you the reason why I leave the sliced surface at the top white as shewn in the drawing.

Sometimes you will see your float tilt up and lie down flat on the top of the water. That indicates that a fish has sucked up your bait, and raised it so much off the bottom that, the weight being taken off, the float no longer rides partly *immersed*, but lies flat. It means that the bait is in the fish's mouth. Strike immediately. But this is very rare.

Sometimes when they are very wary the depression of the float will be of the slightest, so slight that you could not detect it but for the alternate white and red bands, or from the float being on tilt and approaching towards the perpendicular, this continues, and some time after there comes just one twitch of a sixteenth of an inch seemingly in depth. It is most difficult to see, and impossible unless the water be still. Strike for it. It is not a bob, but a distinctly jerky twitch. Very good fish are taken on no more.

But you will not strike for so little unless you are driven to it. You will first expect the rapid succession of well marked jerky twitches, and you will wait patiently for them, the Labeo being frequently a very slow biter. Sometimes the interval between the first gentle movements of the float, and the arrival of the moment when you may strike, covers some minutes, it seems at the time to be hours; sometimes, but not so often, they take you by surprise by commencing to twitch immediately.

So much do the Labeo bites vary that it is a great advantage to fish two or three in company, and help each other by comparing notes from time to time, as you sit side by side fishing within two or three yards of each other. So much do the Labeo bites vary that when one gets a fish, and the others have missed their bites, practised fishermen are not ashamed to ask each other what did you strike for, not that they do not know how Labeo bite, but that they wish to reassure themselves of the variation of bite on at the time. Also it is a great encouragement to see a man to right or left of you get into a good fish. It tells you that the fish are there, and that if you will take sufficient pains to be unwearingly watchful till the first move comes, then intensely prepared till the critical second comes, and then instant to strike during that very second. It tells you that if you can screw yourself up to this tension you too may be fast into a whopper. I have warned you above against losing confidence in yourself, and I know you will do it in spite of the warning. Indeed I should not be a bit surprised if you went further and laid the blame to the bites having been wrongly described. No amount of letter press will teach a man the bites said one of the last fishing party. You can only give the typical bites said another. And when you have told them everything, and they come to putting it in practice, and sit by the water and miss bite after bite as we have done, they will only say you are lying, said a third.

Still further to illustrate the difficulty of the fishing I may mention that on one occasion three of us were fishing together, sometimes within a foot of each other, never more than three yards apart. All the morning from 7 to 11 B and C could do nothing and thought the fish weren't biting, till they saw A fast into one good fish after another, besides breaking hook hold on others, in short having a very fine time of it. Then they asked him what he was striking for and he told them exactly, but they had lost confidence in themselves, and could not get hold of the fish at all. Breakfast over and we were at it again before 2 P.M. The fortunes were changed, A could not tackle them, while B hit it off admirably. C was not present. Another morning it was C that made the bag, and A and B were out of it. And yet A, B and C were no novices at this particular sort of fishing, but men that knew their business well. There was no accounting for it except on the theory that this class of fishing needs extreme tension to be even with its difficulties and that sometimes you can do it, sometimes you cannot, however much you try to pull yourself together. How do you account for it that an ordinary non-professional can one day play a better game of billiards than usual, and another day cannot hit a ball for the life of him? Analyzed it is the state of the non-professional's intestinal canal that has affected his eye, and he can't get the better of it do what he will on those days. Even the professional is not altogether superior to such subtle influences of matter over mind, but he has minimized them by such constant practice that he has approximated to the precision of an unthinking machine, and without much effort of mind effects, almost mechanically, what has become an easy matter-of-course to him. And so it is in this fishing. N, of whom mention is made above, fished so frequently for these fish that he was practically a professional, and the precision with which he struck his fish was marvellous, whereas all the rest of us vary day by day in our success in striking. I don't say that the remedy is an antibilious pill before fishing, but I do warn you, that the proper strike is not "as easy as lying."

If these are the difficulties of one who knows when he ought to strike, the difficulties in accomplishing what you know is right and wish to do, how much worse is the position of those who have but hazy notions of when they ought to strike, or have not the light rod and sensitive float necessary to aid them in accomplishing the refinement of skill. One of such told me that if he caught one fish in two hundred bites it was all he could do. And yet he sticks to it. Poor fellow, I shall not be happy till I have taken him in hand and made a man of him.

These are typical Labeo bites, and it took us years to find them out, and I may as well tell you how it was done, that you may have the more confidence in their being rightly described, and having confidence that you are striking rightly, may be the more likely to get sport. In 1881 your humble servant wrote Chapter XII of *The Rod in India* on Bottom fishing for Labeo and White Carp. It fell into the hands of N and E, inseparables and both keen fishermen, and started them. N's speciality was that he was a good roach and barbel fisherman in England, so his education was all in the right direction; and he had leisure, and the very best of opportunities, for close to him were tanks full of Labeo, one square built tank being a quarter of a mile on each side, and another not a very great deal less, besides others covering an acre or so. And so of course he was constantly fishing, and watching the natives fish, and observing when they struck, and yet it took them years to advance beyond what they found in "*The Rod in India,*" which was founded on very much less ample opportunities of observation. Then they tumbled across this child, and like right good fellows, as fishermen always are, compelled me to come fishing with them, and the result was, as I have told you, 678 lbs. to 4 rods in 3 days. Since then I have laid others in, and by much combined expenditure of brain tissue, and experimentalising, we have added one little wrinkle after another. Your humble servant added some things, that poaching son of "San Pathrick," others, and so on. But though all these wrinkles be told you, and even shewn you in practice at the water's side, still it will be many a long day before you can acquire the marvellous rapidity of eye and hand, with the self confident decision, which N had. At this peculiar style of fishing he was a wonderful performer. I never saw his equal at it. He it was who single handed beat the three of us by taking 361½ lbs. out of the 678, or more than half the whole bag to his single rod. So if you can't do the same all at once lay the blame not on this book please, but on the performer, your good self.

Having thus worked at it for years, and watched natives, and fished together, and consulted together, the manner of biting was reduced to writing as exactly as possible from memory, and there it was kept till the next fishing trip, and there it was compared with actuals at the water's side, and touched up and completed in camp while the eye and mind were freshly impressed with every detail. And yet I must add that all I can aim at giving the reader is the typical bites. There will still remain variations on which the angler must exercise his discretion, sometimes almost striking on the chance. Still if you study and follow the typical bites given you, the rest will come in time as matter of experience, and let me strongly advise you to err in the direction of patiently seeing a Labeo bite through, waiting long for expected twitching, and suffering your bait to be stolen again and again, rather than too early taking to striking on the chance. That striking on the chance can only be had recourse to by an expert who knows when he is driven to it as a last resource and when not. And even what some of us call striking on the chance would not be so called by a first class professional like N. I have seen him strike a good fish and say "there you couldn't have seen that."

But there is one more essential in the 'strike,' which has been alluded to above, but had best be re-impressed in this connection, and that is that it must be a good deal harder than for roach. My excuse for repetition is that I have found it necessary, having sat by a man who did not take long before he became a capital hand at it, but who nevertheless had to be told of it again and again before he would be convinced, and confessed that it had gone sadly against the grain to give up the light 'strike' to which he had trained himself in youth. The 'strike' must be hard enough to break drawn gut for a certainty, and generally to break medium trout gut. And this strength of 'strike' is best both for Labeo and White Carp. The Olive Carp has a mouth of a different character and a gentler 'strike' will do for him, but as he ordinarily pokes his nose in among his betters he must be content with the same strike as they get. It won't hurt him.

These are Labeo (*Shèl-kendai* in Tamil) bites of which we have been speaking, and the bites of the White Carp (*Veng-kendai* in Tamil and classically *Cirrhina cirrhosa*) and of the Olive Carp (*Shàni-kendai* in Tamil and scientifically *Barbus chrysopoma*) are very similar, so similar that it will take you some time to tell them apart, and not without long practice can you feel at all certain. This adds another charm to the fishing, the not knowing for certain, and hazarding a guess as to what fish is at you. Directly you have hooked your friend you can make a shrewder guess, but still not a certainty by any means, for the White Carp, (*Cirrhina cirrhosa*), which is cousin-german, you will remember, to the well known, the splendid Mirga (*Cirrhina mrigala*) of Bengal, makes a more active fight; but the Labeo often run larger, so some prefer one, some the other. The Olive Carp (*Barbus chrysopoma*) ranks many a step below the other two; still he is not to be despised when he tumbles in amongst the others.

Still there is a difference in the bites that in time you may come to recognize. The Olive Carp's bite is given above as most dissimilar, as one would naturally expect from the different formation of its mouth. The White Carp's mouth is, like the Labeo's, placed not in front, but under the snout, though not quite so markedly as in the Labeo, consequently the manner of biting is very similar. But ordinarily the White Carp is a bolder biter than the Labeo, commencing his rapid twitching at once, without any of the premonitory fumbling of the Labeo. When he does you can't strike too soon. The earlier you strike the better your chance. It is quicker fun than with the Labeo. The waiting for the Labeo's bite to develop from slow fumbling to rapid twitching is often very taxing to the patience, and impatience has to be paid for in the loss of your fish.

While we are on bites it may be as well to remember how to distinguish the bite of a prawn from that of a fish. The prevailing characteristic of it is slowness without ever a twitch in it. Out go his two great arms and slowly, slowly draw the bait to his mouth. It is slowly, slowly therefore that your float descends; slowly, slowly it goes up and down, and then it is sometimes carried along the bottom, but always slowly, slowly without ever a marked twitch in it.

Crabs also will take your bait but they pull it down less, and their movement along the bottom is slower still.

How to distinguish the bite of small fish is more difficult. The young of Labeo and White Carp bite just like their elders, only a trifle less cautiously. The bite of young fish is as a rule always more imprudent than the bites of those who have come to years of discretion. It is the old story "Fools rush in where angels fear to tread." But the bite of the Chela and the innumerable little carp of an inch or two long that crowd round your bait and knock it to pieces before the big fish come on the scene and warn them off, is easily distinguishable. In shallow water you may see how they go to work. They make a dash at your bait and nip a little tiny bit out of it. By their movements they seem to knock it out, but the marks on the bait show they nip it out. Stand in the water with bare legs and you will feel their tiny nips. But the result on the float is just as if they had knocked it out. The float moves suddenly and slightly from one side to the other, there is no downward movement at all, just as if the lower end of it had had a smart little tap, just as if a tiny fish had run against or kicked it. There is nothing for it but to let them have their game till their movements have served to attract the attention of the big fish, and then they'll soon be made to clear out.

When the big Labeo and White Carp are around you they drive off not only the small fish, but also the prawns and crabs. You never get prawns and big fish simultaneously. Though when the good fish cease biting the prawns will come on again. They will play you an interlude; and a doleful business it is.

But who shall tell the delights, the dangers, the anxieties of the Labeo and White Carp bites and strikes. And when told who will believe the tale till he has seen and experienced the reality. I was an unbeliever myself as I have told you (page 3) and so was another of whom I could tell you. He was one who had killed salmon I believe, trout I know, Mahseer too up to 46 lbs., and Carnatic Carp in plenty. He may be taken as a typical unbeliever like myself, one who looked down on, and couldn't bring himself to be bothered with float-fishing. And yet now he is an enthusiast. Where then are you on a higher platform, unbelieving reader mine, that you should presume to condemn what you know nothing whatever about. I tell you it is just as silly as those wise-acres from England that flit a few months through India, and are persuaded they know a great deal more about it than those who have devoted all the best years of a lifetime to it. My answer to such objections is that I don't know a man that has been laid on to this fishing, whatever may have been his fishing antecedents, that hasn't gone mad over it, and if you want *desipere in loco* now's your chance.

E's got a bite; a Labeo bite; you know it by his silence. He answers no questions. Not even a pretty girl could get a word out of him now. He is intently watching his float, with every faculty at the extremest tension waiting for the critical second at which he must strike instanter. You too are watching your float, and can't take your eyes off to look at him or his float, though you are only 6 ft. apart. You hear the rrrug of a strike, as the line gives a peculiar sort of twang of its own, difficult to express with letters, the sound that tells you the line is suddenly as taut as it can bear, down right fast into a good one. The very sound is electrical, still more is the feeling so to him who has struck, and experiences in his own hand that he is well home in something firm that means fighting. Every ounce in that Labeo is game, astonishingly game, not exactly with the rapidity of a trout or a Mahseer, but still with a power of staying that astonishes you. And if you have been missing bite after bite for half an hour there is a special feeling of exultation in being even at last with the thief. E is on his pins sharp, and is edging off to one side with his fish as soon as he can induce it to move away from the fishing spot, because E as we are calling him, though it might be any one else, does not want to get entangled with his friend's lines, or to disturb their fishing, for the odds are they are having bites at the same time. Up springs the attendant with the landing-net, for he too has caught the frenzy. E's tongue is loosened. Take care man, take care, don't go making plunges at him like that, he is not half killed yet, wait till I bring him well in to you. Take care, wait I tell you. There you go, missed him again. Keep clear of the line, you'll break it. Don't be in such a hurry. Don't be excited. Now, now's your time. Missed him again I declare! I'll be bound he'll lose the fish for me! And so on and so on.

There is another bite and a strike, but no results. Missed him, too late for him.

Another bite, and another strike. Ah! I felt him that time.

Another, and the striker is getting warm over his misses as who can help doing. Oh! he's carried off everything. Such a beauty. The finest fish in the tank I verily believe.

And so we go on within easy earshot of each other as the sport proceeds, and taking part in each other's triumphs, disappointments, disasters. Many a line is carried away, many a hook broken at the barb, many a fish lost after hooking, and, last but not least, many a good one landed.

Have I been talking only of Madras fish? No, by no means. All that is in the previous pages is, I believe, practically applicable to all India, Burmah and Ceylon. The White Carp, (*Cirrhina cirrhosa*) is, as I have said, cousin-german to the magnificent Mirga (*Cirrhina mrigala*) of Northern India. The Olive Carp (*Barbus chrysopoma*) is so like *Barbus sarana* that only an expert can tell them apart. The latter is known as *Poti* or *Sărăl-poti* in the vernacular at Calcutta, and I have seen them caught with a hook and line in the Havildar's Tank on the maidān there.

I have little doubt that all the Labeo of Northern, Southern, Western and Eastern India and Burmah may be caught by the same manœuvres, and that the Mirga of Northern India will succumb to the same tactics as his cousin of the south, and that *Barbus sarana* (*Poti* and *Sărăl-poti*) like *Barbus chrysopoma* and a number of other large carp which are common to all the Presidencies, may advantageously be fished for in the same way, with variations perhaps in the size of the hook. But for all the larger carp to wit Rohi, Kàlabous, and all the other larger Labeo, and for Mirga, and his cousin the White Carp, and for the Olive Carp, and all the other innumerable *large* Carp or Barbel of India the No. 1 Limerick hook will do. If you condescend to smaller carp you must lessen your hook.

What a large category of fish this includes, and of how many good sorts, spread, in one form or another, all over India, and Burmah, and probably Ceylon too, would hardly be conceived by any one who has not seen Day's *Fishes of India*, and learnt something of how much more prolific of fish India is than England, as well as how much larger the fish run as a rule. I therefore add a short indicative chapter on this head. The reader is also referred to the same Chapter VIII for such details as descriptive formula, habitat and vernacular names of all the fish mentioned above.

In giving plates I have thought that *Labeo calbasu* is from an angler's point of view sufficiently indicative of all the Labeo, and *Cirrhina cirrhosa* is so like *Cirrhina mrigala* that there would be no advantage in a second plate.

I think so highly of the sensitive qualities of my detective float that I have sent it to Farlow of the Strand for the benefit of English roach fishers, if they are not too conservative to try it.

I am inclined to think also that the Catla (*Catla Buchanani*) could probably be taken in the same way: and if so what grand short he would give, for he runs to 50 and 100 lbs., and is largely kept in ponds in Calcutta. The English soldiers in Calcutta who fished the Havildar's Tank certainly told me that they never caught a Catla with a hook unless by chance they hooked him foul when rubbing against the bait, but the natives there I know catch them fairly, running up to 40 lbs. in the ponds in the Calcutta Zoological Gardens, and I heard it was with a worm; but the net caught one of 50 lbs. which I examined in Calcutta in 1883, it had pharyngeal teeth, and nothing but green food in its stomach, both indications that it should not be above a paste bait, and what business had it rubbing against the soldier's paste bait, as they said, if it did not mean taking it.

I heard of one old fisherman in particular *cognomine* Jones, who used to catch them weekly with paste, and when they would not take an ordinary paste bait his infallible recipe was to mix eggs of red ants with the paste. But this is hearsay through a third party; I never met the individual himself. I heard he had crossed the Styx. May be you'll think he's mythological. I cannot think so because the man who told me was a right good fellow and of course a fisherman; as keen as Keane's mustard.

I could very much wish I had a chance of trying in the hot weather and rains whether my detective float wouldn't put me on terms with the Catla. Will some one try and tell me? He has only to fish as if for Labeo, and look out he is not broken if he hooks a Catla. The older and bigger the fish the wiser and the warier. It is the same with some of us. And with the fish it is a case of survival of the wariest. His wariness has saved him.

A thing or two more may well be made a note of in connection with the Labeo and White Carp bites. You will do well to sit right down on a level with the water for you can see them much better when on a level with your float, than when looking down on them from above.

You can do nothing if there is wind and wave. You need still water to see your float. The stiller the better.

The fish are not shy of your coming to the very edge and sitting there. Ordinarily the water is so coloured that they cannot see you on the edge when you are fishing at the depth of 3, 4, or more feet.

The fish are singularly local, and when you have struck and lost your bait they seem to hang about that exact spot for preference, taking your fresh bait much more readily there than if you put it in a yard or less to right or left of the spot.

They do not seem to be scared by your striking, but rather attracted by the broken bits of bait that fall off your hook.

When you are fishing on steps sometimes they will be busy with your bait in a way you cannot strike for, and yet they will gradually push your bait about till it rolls off the step on which you would have it on to a lower one, and the consequence is your float is drawn under by the weight of your bait and lead. You will soon get to know this slower motion from a bite. Do not strike, but gently lift your bait and draw it towards you till it rests again on the step which gives you the proper indicative bottom.

If they are not biting a slight lift of your bait an inch or two letting it fall again quietly will sometimes serve to attract the fish.

You will think one day that you have solved the whole question of bites, and the next day you will find to your astonishment that you are out of it. I can only advise you that the matter has been very carefully thought out, and laid down in this little book, and that the secret of your difficulty is that there are such a variety of modes of biting, and that you *cannot* learn them all at once, but must take time and frequent experiences.

When you see bubbles coming up close to your float, it means that there is a fish at your bait. Look out for him.

It is a great thing to have both Labeo and White Carp in the same pond because one frequently takes up the running handsomely when the other is completely off the feed. Similarly the Olive Carp, though less worthy, serve to fill an interlude at times.

In the fishing for Labeo you will require a good sized landing-net, say 15 inches in diameter, and as the fish are heavy not only must the handle be strong, but it must be held in the right fashion. Your native attendant will always put the net under the fish, and then lift the net at right angles to him, so that the whole weight of the fish is at right angles to the handle. Not the strongest landing-net going can stand that long, the majority will be ruined in a single day's fishing, the weight of the fish bending the iron of the landing-net close up to where it is screwed into the handle. Directly the fish is in the net the handle should be brought into a perpendicular position, and the fish lifted out with the handle all the time perfectly perpendicular. There is then no strain on the iron. There is also no danger of the fish getting out of the net because, if the bag of it is long enough, the fish will fall into the bottom of the net well below the mouth of it, and is really more safely netted than if the net were held out at right angles. Of course you will take the ordinary precaution of putting a small stone into your net first, as it sinks the bag of the net in the water.

The fish is big, and kicks about violently directly he is on shore. Do not attempt to take your hook out till you have killed him, or he may end in hooking you. The English way of killing a fish is to knock or kick him on the head. Straight between the eyes was the old rule at school, and so Englishmen have a natural propensity for sticking to it, but with a fish it is a great mistake. A fish is much more quickly killed by hitting him on the side, and it is so much easier to get at his side, as he flops about on the shore, than at his head. One good blow with the side of the fist, the way a girl hits, on the side of the fish about midships, will burst his bladder, and collapse him at once.

I have forgotten to mention the depth at which to fish. It should not be less than $2\frac{1}{2}$ or 3 feet. You can't expect fish of any size to come and dwell in shallower water. You may see them make a raid in to shallower water and quickly go out again; but they will not trust themselves to stay unless there is such a depth that they feel confident they are not seen. If you can with the point of your rod reach water 3, 4, 5, or 6 ft. deep, so much the better are your chances of big fish. But do not be tempted to throw your bait beyond the top of your rod, because you won't get your fish when he bites, for, as I have said, you can neither see the bite nor strike effectively.

If tempted beyond endurance, as I have been, by seeing fine fish swirling well beyond your fishing point, I have been even with the sons of thieves in this way. I threw out my bait with a swing to where they were, and then kept a taut line on it till I knew from the point of the rod that it must come to where it would rest on the bottom, and my detective float would come into play; the fish followed the falling bait shorewards, my trusty detective signalled all he was up to, and before very long my friend found himself kicking about on shore, till one punch in the ribs reduced him to order.

Did I tell you that the best season is the hot weather, March to October inclusive; the natives say May and June for preference in the Madras Presidency, and I remember that in Calcutta they all told me the same, to wit from May to September inclusive, and specially commended the rains. I was inclined to think at the time that this was because it was only in the cold weather that I could be there. But I have again and again proved it to be correct. The warm weather is the feeding time, and especially when there are showers.

Even in the course of a single day the warmth which accompanies falling rain set them biting at once.

Labeo will bite all day from dawn to dark, but, given no change of weather, they seem to prefer the warmth from 7 or 8 A.M. to 12 or 1 and the evening from 4 or 5 to dark. Fishing all day, as we did, in a tropical sun in the heat of the hot weather you get a *magnificent* thirst on that you would not part with for a five-pound note! They go on biting freely when it is so dark that you cannot see your float, and the best fish seem to get over their shyness then. I therefore wished sorely for a detective float painted with luminous paint. But they do not show far enough off. You can find your matchbox with luminous paint, but not your Labeo.

A word more about their manner of play. I have said their fight is a long and dogged one, game to the last, and you may very easily lose your fish if you do not play him carefully. But now and then you have a fish that rushes straight out to the middle the moment he is hooked, and makes a regular rush of it. That is always a big one and no mistake; and the odds are he breaks you. If you are even with such an one you are a right good fisherman, and your tackle is all sound, and everything runs free.

If your fishing party consists of several you will find it advantageous for two or three to fish side by side, because you get the fish more round you. We have fished three together with not more than eight or ten feet between each, and one on each side was playing a fish, while the one in the middle was having a bite. That was a right good biting day. I would always rather have another man fishing near me than fish alone. The quantity of bait stolen, as well as the quantity scattered every time you strike prematurely, tends to bring fish about, and a fish that has successfully stolen your bait with impunity is not easily scared by your striking. I had one gentleman, of 5 lbs. if I remember rightly, who had been one too many for me bite after bite, till at last, when

I caught him, he was downright "crowded" with bait. More than three anglers is awkward, for directly the fish is struck he should, if large, be politely conducted away from the fishing spot, so as not to disturb it, and played and landed elsewhere. Your personal interview should be strictly private.

If two or three of you are fishing side by side you should, in fairness to each other, all fish at the same depth, or you will find that when you have got the fish together, the majority and the biggest will give the preference to the bait that is in the deepest water, simply because they are shy of coming into shallow water. Nevertheless do not be tempted to fish with your float any further out than exactly under the point of your rod. For instance if you are fishing off steps you should all fish with your baits resting on the same step, as you will find the fish will congregate about that step, and be chary of coming in to one nearer shore and not so deep. Besides being fair play, it will add to the aggregate of general sport that all who are fishing side by side should fish at the same depth.

The size of bait we used was enough to well cover the hook, say a little more than the size of your thumb nail. Some used a lump as big as the end joint of the thumb, as being more attractive, but when once you have got the fish about you I don't think it is an advantage. It only takes them longer to get outside it, and all you want is to conceal the whole of your hook.

That poaching son of Holy St. Dennis introduced a very unholy addition. Besides his No. 1 Limerick hook baited like ours he had another bare hook of the same size hanging below his baited hook, with an inch of gut between the hooks. As the bait was always resting on the ground the extra bare hook lay of necessity well upon the ground also, and so was not noticeable seemingly, for the fish seemed to bite none the less for its presence. I suppose that practically it was hidden in the mud by its own weight. The result was that he caught some on this extra hook that he failed to hook on his baited hook. Surely he would have been run in for it in England as "Snatching." But he is still at large.

Such things have happened as a Freshwater Shark (*Wallago attu*), and other siluroids of 6 and 7 pounds weight, being taken by this bait, but it is not the proper bait for them, as you will see hereafter, and you are not to expect them. But what you may expect are freshwater turtles. They very commonly take a paste bait, and their bite is just like a fish's; but from the moment you have a turtle hooked there is no longer any mistake. It makes no direction of its own, to right or left or away, as a fish would; it simply strives to keep to the bottom, and offers the dead wobbling resistance any plate or disc would in the water.

But there are turtles and turtles. The black-bellied (*Emys trijuga* or pond tortoise, Tamil *Pī-āmai*) one is as redolent as the worst municipal drain in the country, and yet it has a way of coming out of the water as if it were a very impersonation of guileless innocence, "I tell you I'm all green fat" it whispers softly as it is being hauled out, but when you have it on land, and are stooping to take out the hook, then suddenly there is emitted a knock-me-down odour fetid, fetid, fetid beyond description. Fishing with a friend who fished as a man should, with his brains, and who, being a man of education and observation, turned his enquiring mind on to everything new, I had one of these black-bellied tortoises on. Directly I saw his black belly emerging from the water I knew his tricks and his manners in spite of the unctuous green-fat smile he put on. "Oh what's that?" eagerly asked my friend with the enquiring mind. "Take it to the Saib, take it to him immediately" I said, as I carefully swung it inland as far as ever I could from myself. His thirst for knowledge was satiated in an instant, and though he is a member of a learned profession, my firm belief is that he has never enquired about anything since. That one awful stench has ruined him professionally. Write over him, 'Promising medico spoilt by a turtle.'

But as I have said there are turtles and turtles, the white-bellied one (*Emyda granosa*, the freshwater turtle, Tamil *Pālāmai*) is the real Simon pure. He must be treasured and made into soup. So excellent is he that I hope to make experiments in domesticating and breeding him for the table. The following is the recipe of a friend well known in these parts as a good fisherman and a good cook and a good fellow :—

Recipe.—" To cook the yellow-bellied turtle soup kill the animal by cutting the throat; remove the viscera, &c.; put all the flesh and fat on a dish; boil the shell and feet in a little water, taking off any scum that rises to the surface; strain this liquor and put it away. Make a basis for your soup from sheep's head and a few feet. Put in a bunch of herbs; flavor with salt and put in a few forcemeat balls. Now put in the turtle flesh and boil it in the liquor obtained from the sheep's head and feet, adding the fluid got from the turtle's shell and fins. Cut up all the green fat into square pieces, and throw in a glass of Madeira. Thicken if you like with cornflour or isinglass. The turtle makes a most delicious curry."

While quoting my friend's recipe for turtle soup I may as well append a few other fish cooking recipes that he has kindly given me, for I find that whenever my soul swells rapturously on the memory of magnificent sport, and I commence dilating grandiloquently thereon, some mundane mind is sure to stop me with the utterly non-pertinent question " Is it good to eat ?" You might as well ask me of a brilliant break at billiards " Is it good to eat ?" I find such silly questions very annoying. So I will stop the mouths of all such materialists by the following recipes from the same excellent authority :—

Recipe.—" Gudgeons are best fried. They should be eaten the day they are caught. Don't remove the head; it is gelatinous and delicious; clean and dry them; dip them in beaten egg; cover them lightly with fine bread crumbs, salt, &c.,

and fry quickly. A little ketchup or lime juice is good with them."

Recipe.—"Any gelatinous fish is excellent this way. Fill a small pie-dish with gudgeons, or any small fish, or slices of fish, interspersing layers of sliced onion, pepper, salt, and tomatoes. When the dish is nearly full pour in vinegar until the fish are covered; put a piece of buttered paper over the top; and bake for half or three-quarters of an hour. This is a good dish, and will keep cold for several days. Small trout, sprats, or herrings done so at home are most delicious.

N.B.—The stewing or baking apply to almost any fish, but more particularly to those of a gelatinous nature."

And now for another reeipe. "How to eat a Murral?" That's my friend's Irish heading I may tell you in strict confidence for how to cook a murral, but don't let out I told you, or may be he'll be after shillalying me the next time we meet at the club.

Recipe.—"A Murral is an excellent fish if properly cooked. Take one weighing about 2 lbs.; remove the head and all the viscera; wash carefully and dry; now fill him with well made veal stuffing, *i.e.* bread crumbs, thyme, butter, pepper, and salt; lay him in a shallow pie-dish with a cupful of good gravy, and a good lump of butter; surround him with a bed of tomatoes, and bake three-fourths of an hour. It can be eaten hot or cold."

Another plan. **Recipe.** "Boil a good sized murral; remove all the meat and smash it up in a soup plate with a fork; allow it to get cold; mix in salt, black pepper, a good lump of butter, a table spoon of mushroom ketchup, and one claret glassful of milk. Make hot in a saucepan, stirring it occasionally. This is a most excellent dish. Any cold fish is delicious prepared in this way."

One of those objectionable doubters that will get in your way stumbled across my friend of the recipes, and questioned whether there really was any fishing in a certain locality.

The latter promptly shut him up with "Why mon! there's eels you could fly a kite with." And this is the way he cooks them.

Recipe.—"Eels are good in curries, pies, or stewed. It is a mistake to skin small eels; first give them a half boil; pour away this water, and add as much as will cover them. The eels should be in junks about two inches in length. Put in plenty of pepper, salt, a slice of lemon, and one small onion chopped up. Stew very gently until tender; then add some flour and butter to thicken the same. Lower the lights and have a little slow music in the next room when partaking of stewed eels or turtle soup."

Mindful of the wise saw first catch your hare, I shall have to tell you by and bye how to catch the said gudgeon, murral and eels; the turtle you know already; and how to swing the black-bellied ones to your friends. They'll never forget you if you do, and after all it is a simple and inexpensive way of living in their memories.

Prawns will sometimes trouble you. When they do it is a terrible nuisance. The moment your bait is on the bottom they steal it. You may know them by the bite above described (page 46). In Calcutta I have seen the natives fishing purposely for them. They use a hook about the size of a roach hook, and a bit of prawn for bait. The hook is so small that the prawn passes it into its mouth, and the stroke is made, not with a twitch as for fish, but with a steady tauten and lift out. They give them plenty of time, waiting till the float has been held well under some little time and is being moved off with. If they used a still smaller hook, say a minnow hook, they would probably do a great deal better. Some Indian prawns, as *Palemon carcinus* of the Indian seas and the Ganges, attain a foot in length, so one can well understand their being fished for for food. Six and a half inches long is a common size in Madras. Still our point is not so much to catch them as to get rid of them. I have managed it in this way. Trading on their preference for animal matter I have shot a couple of crows, or got the entrails of a fowl, and tieing them to a stone, dropped them in near where we were fishing. The prawns gather on to this and leave your bait unmolested. But you cannot do this in water that is used for drinking purposes.

Catching large numbers of fish, as one does in this Labeo fishing, a Salter's circular spring balance will be found a convenient thing for weighing them. "It weighs by ounces up to 30 lbs.," there is a meat hook for the long lumbering Freshwater Sharks, and the scale-pan will give you any fine Labeo's weight separately, while all of a pound or two and under can be piled up in the scale and weighed off in heaps without loss of time.

It will doubtless interest my readers that I should here give the following extracts from letters to "*The Asian*" showing as they do the opinions of other writers on Labeo fishing and supporting my contention that it is to be had elsewhere than in the Madras Presidency :—

I can assure "H. S. T." that I have taken "Rohu" with fish bait and with shrimps.

They were tank fish, and about 4 lbs. in weight. The bait used was a small fish known as the "Derwah." I was not fishing for "Rohu," having always thought that they would not take a fish bait, and to my surprise caught about 15 of them during three days' fishing.

* * * * * *

MEADE SHELL.

TIRHOOT, 14*th April* 1882.

DEAR SIR,

I will try and send H. S. Thomas, through you a sketch of the "*Deruah,*"* or send one in spirits for him. He asks if the *Rohu* is a free biter or fox. During 20 years' experience I have found them both. Sometimes they will manage to take the bait off the hook without hardly moving the float, and at times will drag the rod out of your

* A specimen kindly sent in spirit turns out to be *Nuria danrica.*—H. S. T.

hands if you are not quick enough. The "*Mirka* or *Nain*," a silver fish with salmon-coloured fins, is also a *Labeo*, and is decidedly a fox. It grows to the same size as the *Rohu*, and usually begins to fight when you think you are about to land him. The Cutlah is a grand fish for sport if you can hook him. Some time back I asked in the *Asian* for a bait for Cutlah. I have tried flies, but never succeeded in catching them. The natives say Cutlah will take gram soaked and strung on a thread, and wrapped round a large hook.

There are two more fish, of the *Labeo* species I think, which somewhat resemble the *Rohu*. They are a little shorter bodied and have feelers on the lips. One is of a more golden tinge over the scales, and the other is darker. Both give excellent sport. The first is known in Behar as the "*Kohn*," and the second as the "*Kalabans*."

MEADE SHELL.

TIRHOOT, 15*th June* 1882.

THE ROHU.

I have intended for some time sending you a few notes on fishing, but the weather has been so depressing that I have been unable to summon up sufficient energy to write.

Imprimis allow me, though rather late in the day, to thank Mr. Thomas for his kindness in replying to some queries of mine inserted in the *Asian* about 2½ months ago regarding the "*Rohu*" species.

I have since then both caught myself, and seen caught by my fishing chums, some very fine specimens, notably the following :—

One fish of		7	lbs.,	caught by	Yuba Bill.
,,	,,	9	,,	,,	,,
,,	,,	11	,,	,,	,,
,,	,,	18	,,	,,	,,
,,	,,	16	,,	,,	"Tiddu."
,,	,,	14	,,	,,	"Robert."

Tiddu, allow me to remark, is not a native, as the name would imply, but the proprietor of the water in which the three last-named fish were caught. This water is a splendid lake of unknown depth, and, strange to say, very clear—an unusual thing with Indian lakes and tanks. It had not been fished in for 15 years, until I attracted Tiddu's notice to the enjoyment to be obtained from the gentle art, since which he has become one of its most ardent followers. All the fish herein specified were caught by paste, and some of them gave splendid play; the second in the list, 9 lbs. in weight, jumped out of water clean over a curved branch over which I had to play him, until I sent a man up the tree to bend it down level with the water. This branch was, by *measurement fairly taken* after the fish was landed, 2 feet 11 inches above the surface of the water. Mr. Thomas asks if rohu are worth preserving: after this I hope he will think they are. I do not think they are generally predaceous in spite of a few instances hitherto quoted by your correspondents. I have spun in waters where they have been plentiful, and have used live bait, catching murrell and other predaceous fish but no *rohu.* The latter I have never caught with anything but paste (attar), and I prefer the white to the brown flour for this purpose. I think as a general rule rohu bite very gently, and it is as well to let the float go well under or move along the surface before striking. By the bite or rather nibble, it is difficult to know whether a large or small fish is at the hook. They generally spring out of water or rush along the surface when hooked, but I have known some of them hang like a lump of lead, especially the 18-pounder in the list above noted. This fish came straight to the surface and allowed me to tow him quietly along for fifty yards to a favourable landing place, and then fought like a demon for about twenty minutes. They evidently grow at a good pace when unmolested by predaceous fish. In a small tank, previously empty, I placed a few rohu about four inches long, three years ago. This tank is fed from a canal by a very small cut, which would let in nothing above ½ lb. in weight, and on trying it three or four times last month I caught a few very clean fish from three to four pounds in weight.

I think rohu are the most compactly built fish in existence, tremendously thick behind the head, and very heavy for their length. They generally give very fair sport, although their comparatively narrow fins and tail do not allow them to make the prolonged rush of the mahseer. I would certainly recommend Mr. Thomas to include them in his stock of new fish for the Madras preserves. They are very nice eating.

The *kalbans* is a fish that does not, as a rule, run over 5 or 6 lbs., of an ugly dark colour, with bright pink or magenta eyes, and worth nothing for eating; he gives better sport than a rohu for his size, though not so thickly built.

The mirgah is a most symmetrical fish and very clean looking. I have never caught one over 7 lbs., and have only seen one over that weight; that one however was about 15 lbs. He plays well and is generally nice eating though occasionally muddy.

I have put together these few notes from my shikar diary, and I shall be only too glad if they are of any use to Mr. Thomas.

I had almost forgotten to mention that the small mouth, looking as if sewn up at the sides, of these fish, i.e. *rohu*, *kalbans*, and *mirgah*, precludes the possibility of their being generally predaceous, although they may possibly be so if short of food.

YUBA BILL.

Referring now to the article, (also in your last issue) by "Rod," I quite agree with him that temperature has quite as much to do as clearness of water with mahseer fishing. Give me a good warm day in May, June, July, or even a couple of months later, after rain, and a good stout rod, or "luggie" and double salmon line, and if I would not be happy,—why nothing scarcely could make me so; only see well beforehand to your spoons and swivels, and be your motto "tourjour près" when the "tug of war" comes. About fishing in the old country I cannot say much, as it is so long since I was there unfortunately, but I have done a little in that way all over Bengal and the North-west Provinces, and believe firmly that it is absolutely loss of time to fish for *rohi*, *cutla*, or that noble fish the *mirga*, except in the rain. Even the natives laugh at you if you attempt to, but the *murral* or *sowl* I have frequently caught in the cold weather, but never one weighing more than 5½ seers or 11 lbs.

The finest tank fishing I ever had was some three years ago in the Serie tank, near Chupra, district Sewan, where in two hours a friend and I landed fish weighing one maund and 28½ seers; these we weighed on our way home in the jail there. Oh! but for a week there again next rains, along with some of my "Blue" friends who I often think of, and who are as fine a set of planters as in India—I care not where.

The tank when I went there the natives said was charmed; anyhow, after obtaining permission to fish there from the Collector, I proved that I was the charmer.

Many a big one I have run fairly for a good half hour there with the reel whistling every now and then, and the silk line I used running out so fast that it actually cut the skin pretty deep in my fingers.

Up there too, fly-fishing for "chelwas" is very fair sport. The well known "Ned" is the boy there to take you flying through water in his elegant dog cart up to your axles in water, and also to give you an A. I. sucking pig and a bottle of "Phiz" for dinner, and a hearty welcome; if any man could want more than that, I pity him.

TURPIN.

TANK FISHING FOR RAHOO AND MIRKA.

DEAR SIR,

Referring to the letters of "Rod" in your paper of 13th ultimo, and of "Turpin" and "Yuba Bill" in your last, it may interest them and others to know that it is easy to get *rahoo* and *mirka* to take a bait in tanks throughout the cold weather if the tank is well baited.

I have very frequently caught these fish (even when there has been a slight frost during the night) in the cold weather, by well ground-baiting a tank for two or three days. The bait consisted of linseed roasted to a nice coffee color, and oil cake (mustard seed) broken into small bits and similarly roasted. These are mixed with earth, and made into lumps about the size of a cricket ball, and should be thrown into the tank twice a day just where you mean to fish. A few leaves of the getmun plant, which resemble the toulsee, and has a somewhat similar scented leaf, may be added to the ground-bait. The deepest part of the tank should be selected, and the bait, which may be paste, earth-worm, or wasp grub, should be two or three inches off the ground. Undoubtedly the best time for fishing for these fish, and all the carp tribe, is from July to 15th November, but it is quite possible to have good sport in the cold season.

MEADE SHELL.

TIRHOOT, *2nd March* 1883.

I doubt if a paste bait can be found more simple, cleanly and effective than the one recommended on page 32. Still as ground-nut may not always be procurable I suppose I must give alternative possibilities.

In my earlier fishing days I used the native cocoanut rice cakes (Tamil *āppam*) and that may be reverted to. But it is not so good.

In the absence of ground-nut the following compromise may also be tried :—

Boiled rice ground fine 2 parts.

Coriander roasted and ground fine 1 part.

Bran Q. S., or as much as may be wanted to bring the bait to a proper consistency. (See page 33 *supra*).

The following elaborate baits were kindly given me in Calcutta by one who was named to me on many hands as an authority, but I must premise that I have no personal knowledge of their efficacy or otherwise :—

GROUND BAIT FOR FISHING.

"*Mattee*" seeds, or Fenugreek, one seer.

"*Aik Angee*," one seer.

"*Thumbul*," half seer.

"*Kala Sorsoo*," or Black mustard seeds, half seer.

"*Goda Butch*," or Sweet Flag, one chittack.

Partially roast or broil these ingredients on a heated shovel or earthen flat pan, till the aroma is sensibly smelt at a distance of 8 or 10 paces in the direction of the wind. While still hot pound in a mortar to a fine powder. Mixing the lot well together keep in a wide mouth stoppered bottle for use.

Use as follows :—

A table spoonful or two is mixed with 6 or 8 fistsful of soft wet clay at the tank side, and made into balls the size of a pigeon's egg; throw a dozen or so of these balls into the tank, only about the spot you intend to cast your hook, and as close together as possible. Your hook should lie a foot or cubit in advance of the ground thus baited.

Baits.

Rice flour mixed with a little water; the dough formed is placed between 2 or more betel or pan leaves and baked on an open fire till it becomes stiff and pasty; take a pinch of the paste and roll it between the fingers to the shape and thickness of a worm and cover the hook with it, point barb and half the length of the shaft. Cast in your hook as directed to a foot or cubit in advance of the ground bait. While thus waiting for a bite the fish are further drawn towards the spot by a wet mixture of rice finnings "*Kooroe*" made into balls of a smaller size than the ground bait, and thrown with a dash close to the float at intervals of 5 or 10 minutes and oftener, as the fish get about the place, to cloud the water and hide your line.

Earthworms—"*Ketchwah.*"

The larvæ from a wasp's nest—"*Boltha chack.*"

Bread formed into a stiff paste with cheese a little butter or milk, or in place of cheese ants' eggs "*Peepra deem*" when procurable is considered the most tempting bait.

Small shrimps—"*Chota Chingree.*"

And almost all flour cake that will bake to a stiff sticky paste may be used.

I give the above recipes exactly as they were given me by one whom I understood to have a high reputation as a fisherman in Calcutta. Still as the orthography has puzzled me a little I will try and work it out for my southern readers who may not be conversant with all the Calcutta terms.

Mattee is doubtless *Mēthī* of Hindustani and Dukhni. It is *Trigonella Fœnum Græcum* which has the following synonyms :—

Arabic.—*Hulbah.*
Persian.—*Shanbalīd. Shamlīt. Shamlīz.*
Tamil.—*Venthayam.*
Telugu.—*Mentulu.*
Malayalim.—*Ulava. Ventayam.*
Canarese.—*Mēnthyā.*
Bengali, Sanskrit, Mahratti, Guzratti,—*Mēthī.*
Cingalese.—*Uluva.*
Burmese.—*Pe-nān-ta-zi.*

Aik Angee is surely *Hing* or *Assafœtida*, a very popular smelling ingredient for ground bait. Its synonyms are

Arabic.—*Hiltīt.*
Persian.—*Angōzah. Angush-gandah.*
Hindustani.—*Hīng.*
Dukhni.—*Hing.*
Tamil.—*Kāyam. Perungāyam.*
Telugu.—*Inguva.*
Malayalim.—*Perungāyam. Kāyam.*
Canarese.—*Ingu.*
Bengali.—*Hing.*
Sanskrit.—*Hinguhu. Rāmatham.*
Mahratti.—*Hing.*
Guzratti.—*Hing. Vagārni.*
Cingalese.—*Perunkāyam* or *Perrungāyam.*
Burmese.—*Shīnkhu* or *Shīngu.*

What *Thumbul* may stand for beats me and all my friends, but surely we have savoury smells enough without it!

Kala Sorsoo is I conjecture Indian mustard *Sinapis Juncea* Linn: *Sinapis Ramosa* Roxb: for which Moodeen Sheriff's Supplement to the Pharmacopœia of India gives the following synonyms:—

Arabic.—*Khardal.*
Persian.—*Sipandān. Ispandān.*
Hindustani and Dukhni.—*Rāī Rāyān.*
Tamil.—*Kadugu.*
Telugu.—*Avālu.*
Malayalim.—*Katuka.*
Canarese.—*Sāsave.*
Bengali.—*Rāi.*
Sanskrit.—*Sarshaphaha.*
Mahratti.—*Moharē.*
Guzratti.—*Rāyi.*
Cingalese.—*Abbē.*
Burmese.—*Munniyēn-zi.*

Goda Butch is evidently Bach which is the sweet flag, *Acorus calamus* with the following synonyms:—

Arabic.—*Vajj* or *Vaj.*
Persian.—*Agre-turkī.*
Hindustani.—*Bach.*
Dukhni.—*Gand-kī-lakri. Gan-kī-lakrī Vach.*
Tamil.—*Vashambu.*
Telugu.—*Vasa-vadaja.*
Malayalim.—*Vashanpa.*
Canarese.—*Bajē.*
Bengali.—*Bach. Sappēd-bach.*
Sanskrit.—*Ugra-gandhaha.*
Mahratti.—*Vēkhanda.*
Guzratti.—*Vaj. Vach.*
Burmese.—*Lenhe. Lene. Linhe.*

I was at the trouble to make up this ground bait once and

I found the warning about keeping it in a stoppered bottle is quite unnecessary, for if you do not it will drive you out of the house.

I have given this recipe at length because I found it much sworn by, and some fishermen are so very particular, but I repeat that in my view you want nothing more than the simple and cleanly bait and ground-bait recommended above at page 32.

Before closing this chapter I wish to enter a protest against the way in which anglers are treated. "All men do take a pride to gird at them" and so do ladies too. I will give you an instance. A most respectable harmless old gentleman of my acquaintance was at a picnic. He was "a man more sinned against than sinning." But he was a fisherman, and so it was considered fair game to pull his leg. And they were all in high spirits, and none of them strangers to each other. So three petticoats went for this poor old fisherman, and one propounded a conundrum at him out loud across the impromptu table. "You know all about fish Mr. ——— How do fish kiss?" The dear old man was however equal to the occasion, and quick as thought replied urbanely "I'll show you, Madam, with the greatest pleasure." But a wiser head remarked that it was fishically impossible, and so the tauntress "declined to take lessons."

Having written the above I had my doubts whether tauntress was not a word of my own coining, so I looked it up in Webster's Dictionary, and found "Tauntress. A female who taunts (*rare*)" I do not think Webster can be right, for they are anything but rare in these parts.

P. S. or P. P. S.—With such a ladylike introduction to an after-thought I may perhaps be allowed to add here, what I cannot now introduce into the right place above, because that part of the book is already irretrievably in print, that since writing the above I have obtained bamboos a very trifle thinner at the point than $\frac{1}{8}$th of an inch in diameter, and that with such a rigid light substance as bamboo you can afford to have the point this mere trifle thinner without sacrificing the advantage of rigidity in striking, and that, short of sacrificing the prime essentials of stiffness and lightness for instant striking, the lighter the rod the more the sport you get out of your fish when playing him. But remember the warning of the Cookery book "first catch your hare," remember that you have to get your fish well hooked before you can play him, and that consequently the former is the more essential point of the two; and in having the point thinner than $\frac{1}{8}$th of an inch you are running it fine whether or not you are losing rigidity and trespassing dangerously on pliability. You certainly cannot run the point as fine as $\frac{1}{16}$th of an inch, you can only go the merest shade finer than $\frac{1}{8}$th and what that shade is, which marks the very border line between luxurious improvement of sport and loss of efficiency in striking power, is a nice point for an expert. For the majority then $\frac{1}{8}$th of an inch is fine enough for your point, but a first class fisherman or a first class tackle maker may be trusted, with bamboo, but only with bamboo, to run it just a shade finer.

And now, in conclusion, I will, for the sake of ready reference, summarize as briefly as possible the angler's requisites for this sort of fishing, presuming that I put down what is the smallest quantity he should take for a week's fishing. After a week's experience he will have learned for himself; and can replenish as he likes, and if money is no great object to him he can always take as much more than I have named as he likes.

Requisites for a week's trip.

1 ten ft. light bamboo rod, (page 16).
1 check winch $2\frac{1}{4}$ inches in diameter.
3 detective floats, (page 23).
30 yards light tussa-silk running-line, (page 21).

2 dozen bare eyed Limerick No. 1 hooks.
3 dozen lengths salmon gut.
Soft lead wire, 2 or 3 yards.
A plummet sinker.
A landing-net, (page 53).
Bait, (page 32).
Ground bait, (page 34).
A knife or scissors.

CHAPTER II.

LIVE-BAIT PICKETING.

VICAR.—Love thy neighbour as thyself friend Dogberry

DOGBERRY.—An' so I do, an't please your worship, so that he doth not go before me a-fishing.

OLD MS.

WHEN fishing for Labeo you will take a few small fish now and then. Select those of about a quarter of a pound, and put them into a bait kettle the moment they are off your hook, using every pains to keep them well and vigorous. Put up your Mahseer, Salmon, or Pike rod, two if you have them, that is any big strong rod with stout running-line; and tie the end of the running-line to a flight of hooks mounted on wire with a double swivel. I use two No. 5 trebles and a No. 1 eyed Limerick as lip hook, the hooks being two inches apart. Then attach a sinker such that a quarter-pound fish cannot move. Nothing is simpler and easier to use than a spherical 12 bore bullet with a hole bored through it. Pass the running-line through this hole in the bullet double, and the bullet through the loop thus formed in the running-line, and pull taut. The bullet can never slip from the position in which you have put it, and is removeable with ease, when you have done fishing. Leave some 2 feet between the bullet and the bait, which you will put on at the last moment, injuring it as little as possible, with the lip hook through the upper lip, and the two trebles each just through the skin on the fish's side. Readers of "*The Rod in India*" will see that this is just a slight adaptation of Colonel Parson's plan of picketing a live bait for Mahseer in coloured water. I have used treble hooks instead of single, and added a second because the Freshwater Shark (*Wallago attu*, *Vále* in Tamil, Assamese *Baralie*) is less

Plate VII

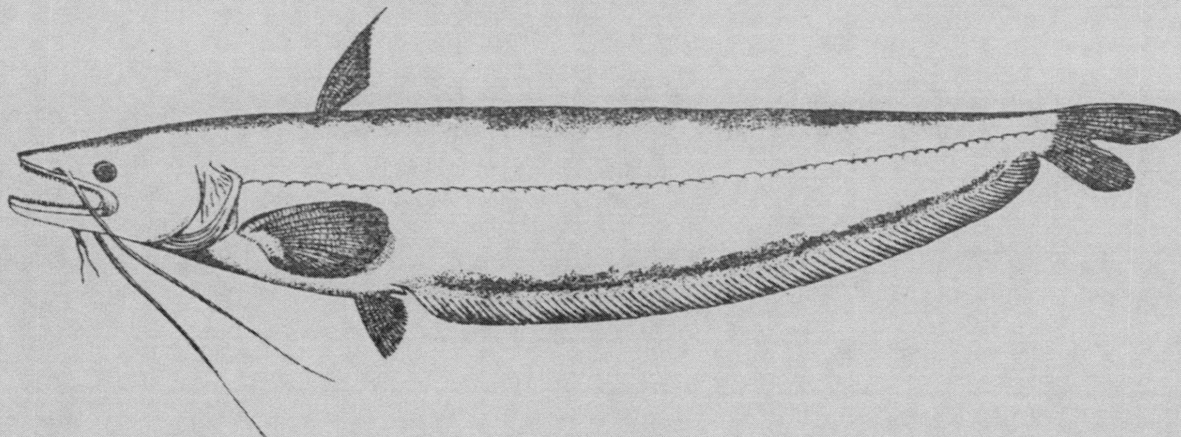

WALLAGO ATTU

likely to be hooked than a Mahseer, as he has not the leathery mouth of the Mahseer, but a terrible mouthful of teeth, against one of which the hook may well come and fail to get a hook-hold. So it is well to add to your chances of hooking by adding an extra hook, as you do with Pike. Still you must not overdo it, as the fish is shy. I have also dispensed with Colonel Parson's precaution of attaching the bullet by a separate thinner piece of cord. This is an excellent precaution of his when fishing for Mahseer, because of the rocks amongst which you find them. But the bottom of a pond is free from rocks, and so you may dispense with it and save yourself trouble. I use wire also because the teeth of the Freshwater Shark would soon cut through gut.

Having thus baited, swing out your bait as far as you can without injuring it, and let it sink. When the bullet is well on the bottom, reel up all the slack line and lay your rod down in a position in which the line will run freely from the point if a fish takes you; and the reel too will work unimpeded. But jam the rod in that position with pegs or stones, or it will be jerked into the water with the first rush of the fish. Put out a rod like this to right and left of you, and go on with your Labeo fishing, till the scream of your reel, or the scream of your attendants, tells you there's a fish on. Instantly chuck down your Labeo rod, and make tracks for your big rod as fast as ever your legs can carry you, for the object is to tauten on to your fish while still he is making his first run, as you cannot tell whether you have a good hook-hold or not, among his many teeth, and your best chance is tautening. You have a heavy rod and strong tackle, so hold on to him all you dare. "If his head doesn't come off I've got him" said a friend. Still he's a big beast running from 4 to 5 and even 6 feet long, and weighing from 10 or 20 lbs. upwards, and though he has none of the rapidity of the Mahseer in their first magnificent rush, still he goes away at a very fair pace like a big steam boat, and now and then he will fling his whole length clean into the air. But it is little more than one spurt and he is beaten, coming in like a great log. A friend was so annoyed at this that as soon as he had his huge fish on shore he "kicked him for being a skunk." Still he is a big fish, and though he may be disappointing in not showing the sport you would expect of one of his size, it is not till *after* he is on shore that you will think of kicking him; up to that you will not be sorry to have him on, and steam boat ways though he has, his very size will awaken excitement enough in all hands, anglers, attendants and spectators till he is successfully brought to the kickable stage.

With this fish I prefer picketing the bait to the bottom to using a float, because the Freshwater Shark frequents the bottom, and because with a line laid out and left to take care of itself there is less entanglement than when using a float. With a float, the bait and the shoreward line both hang from the float, and the former not infrequently twists itself round and round the latter, whereas, with only a bullet, the line from the bullet comes along the bottom of the pond, and the bait swims free above it. Also with a bullet the bait cannot change its position, while with a float it is always working shorewards, and wants more attention in putting it out again from time to time, time that could not possibly be wasted on it if the Labeo are biting freely.

For my own part I would not be bothered to fish for these "skunks," hulking big fellows though they are, except as an adjunct to other fishing. But fished in this way, by an equivalent to a night line attached to a rod and reel, the rod is lying still while you are pursuing other sport, and your men and the villagers delight in the big bit of meat thus acquired for the pot, and got in this way he makes a very pleasant interlude, and however much of an epicure in fishing you may be, you will still find yourself running for your life to get quickly hold of your big rod, when you hear by the scream of the reel, and see by the bending of the top, that a Thames steam boat has got hold of the other end of the line.

I should not omit to mention that you will want a gaff hook to land these fish, and that when landed and carried well away from the water, you will do well to take the precaution of putting the butt of your gaff hook, a big stone, or a log of wood across his jaws before attempting to take out the hook, or you may find that, though lying motionless, and seemingly dead as a door nail, he will suddenly close his awful jaws with a snap, and hold them as firmly closed as a bull-dog's, and you would get a fairly realistic idea of the fine set of teeth he has, all set sloping inwards like a shark's.

I do not believe in gimp in bright Indian waters, because it is so conspicuous, and a shy fish like the Freshwater Shark will not come near it. I therefore use wire in preference. A wire trace is also preferable to a treble gut spinning trace even for Mahseer, because it is very much less visible, indeed I think it is as hard to see as a single salmon gut, while it is incomparably stronger than the strongest treble gut. It is also not liable to rot as gut is. It is moreover much cheaper than gut, and with moderate care one trace will last a lifetime. An objection to it is that it rusts, but this is easily met by laying it up in Vet's Vaseline when out of use. You have to remember also that no wire stands doubling backwards and forwards, therefore avoid haste in straightening out your trace when first setting up, and never try to straighten a kink by forcibly pulling it straight as you might with string. Humour wire in this one matter of never doubling it, and the amount of straight tension it will bear will repay you.

In order to avoid the tendency to rust it is fashionable to suggest the use of copper or brass wire in preference to iron or steel, but a comparison of the relative strengths of different wires should set that question at rest. Accordingly I append an extract from Ganot's Physics, Edition 1875, page 68.

The following table gives the breaking weight in pounds for wire having a sectional area of a square millimetre :—

Antimony cast	1·47
Bismuth	2·13
Lead	4·86
„ drawn	5·19
Tin	6·60
„ cast	9·15
Zinc annealed	31·68
„ drawn	34·58
Gold annealed	24·20
„ drawn	61·60
Silver annealed	36·08
„ drawn	63·80
Platinum annealed	58·85
„ drawn	77·00
Copper annealed	69·52
„ drawn	90·20
Iron annealed	110·55
„ drawn	140·71
Cast Steel drawn	184·36

I therefore prefer steel wire and take the very fine wire commonly used in India for the zitar or native guitar, and readily purchaseable in any bazaar. The diameter of it is ·014 of an inch or No. 28 of Birmingham wire gauge, and a competent authority gives me the breaking weight as 17½ lbs. This is annealed or rendered pliable by heating up to a red heat in charcoal and then cooling *very slowly*. It should take not less than 36 hours to cool, and this cannot be managed without excluding the air by packing it in charcoal dust. The secret of annealing is very slow cooling. With this very fine wire there is a danger of its fusing if you go over red heat, therefore it has to be watched while heating and it is rather a delicate operation.

Having annealed take three lengths and make a twist.

Why not take a wire of treble the size at once and save this trouble of twisting says one. Why? because if there is any flaw in a single wire it is all in one place, whereas in a treble wire you distribute any possible flaws, and cannot have more than one-third of a flaw in one place. Also the very act of twisting eliminates serious flaws, for any wire with such a flaw in it flies while twisting, and the disappointment is to the manufacturer not the fisherman. Also in twisting you stretch one side of the wire and compress the other, with the result that you will find a treble twisted wire will coil up much more easily, and be much less liable to get into kinks than a single wire. A double wire is somewhat simpler to twist than a treble therefore some prefer it. But a treble wire is one-third stronger than a double wire, and is not one atom more visible to a fish. Conceive the thickness of a wire to be represented by a cipher, and placing ciphers side by side in the position which the wires would take in a double and in a treble twist, you will see that there is no more breadth in one case than in the other. It is better therefore to have the additional one-third of strength, as you get it without any sacrifice of visibility, and with additional advantages of pliability and distribution of flaws.

I am told wire may be annealed by boiling in oil. I tried and failed. Perhaps I did not boil long enough, or let it cool slowly enough, by covering up the boiling pot and packing it in saw dust or otherwise when cooling.

For heavy fish then, annealed steel wire is far preferable to either gut or gimp in durability, strength, invisibility and economy. To some minds this last recommendation is the chief one, notably to the hero of the following incident:—Two men who were good fishermen otherwise, meant to go out for the first time after Mahseer, and to take with them a third. The two asked me to procure the proper spoons for them mounted on the best gut. I did. The two knew the value of first class salmon gut and were prepared to pay for it. Not so the third; his soul was horror struck. "You had better return it" he wrote it is so very "expensive it must be human."

A treble wire trace is easily cut to any length with scissors, and as easily fastened to a swivel. But do it so as not to undo the twist in it, or you will weaken it. Pass one end of the treble wire through one eye of the swivel, and keeping about an inch over double it level with the long end and twist the short end round and round the long end close up to the swivel. No further knot is necessary. It will never slip. On no account obtain the twist by holding both wires together and twisting the swivel. That will undo the twist in one of the ends and weaken it. It will also not be so neat.

A convenient way of keeping a twisted wire trace is to put each trace coiled up in a leather pocket of its own. This prevents its springing out, and keeps the Vaseline about it, and it comes out next morning all unrusted and unkinked from its nights lay by.

The above suggestions for the capture of Freshwater Shark (*Wallago attu*) should seemingly be equally applicable to the taking of all the monster Siluroids of different parts of India. I say seemingly because I have not actually taken them with my own hand, and I wish always to make it clear when I am writing from my own knowledge, when on the information of brother anglers, and of course I only quote such information as is in my humble opinion thoroughly reliable, and is also in accord with probabilities deduced from analogy of species within my own knowledge. I allude to such fish as *Bagarius Yarrellii*, the *Goonch* of Northern India, of which there are two plates in *The Rod in India*, one of which is from a photograph of a fish weighing 138 lbs., and measuring 5 ft. 8 inches from the lip to the end of the tail, and 5 feet to the fork of the tail; the circumference of the head being 3 feet 4 inches. The original was caught on a Rohi of 12 or 14 lbs.

Silundia Gangetica is another such monster, called *Gurua* in

Plate VIII

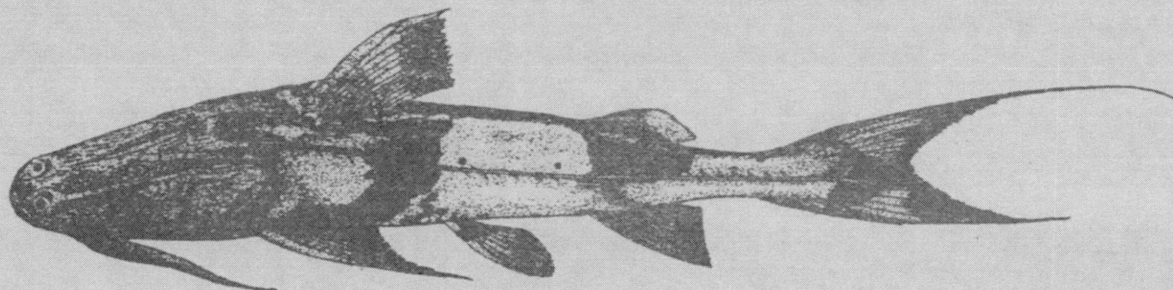

BAGARIUS YARRELLII

Assamese, and said to run to 6 feet in length. I have a record of one of 42 lbs. caught on a spinning tin minnow.

Macrones Seenghala, known as *Shingal* in the northern vernacular is another. I have a diagram of one caught by a correspondent at Gar on the Bheema. And there are others that run to a considerable size. But I will not undertake to say that they will all be found in tanks as well as rivers, as the Freshwater Shark is. There is however a certain amount of presumption in favor of their following river channels into tanks as fry, as others do, if the tanks be in direct connection with such parts of rivers as they frequent.

Here a communication to *The Asian* of 27th February 1883 by *Yuba Bill* will doubtless interest my readers :—

GOONCH FISHING.

I am much obliged to "Rod" for his kindly notice of my enquiries regarding goonch in the penultimate issue of the *Asian*. The fish to which I alluded is, as he suspects, the *Bagarius Yarrelli*, shewn in plate 18, facing page 170, of "*The Rod in India*," and the place is Okhla, seven miles from Delhi.

I generally find the goonch occupying the very head of a rapid; they lie motionless with apparently no effort in the white water among the boulders at the foot of a smooth incline down which the water rushes with immense force through the open sluices of the weir. Some idea may be formed of the strength of the stream from the fact that the river Jumna, which is at this point about three-quarters of a mile wide, is artificially narrowed by a bund to a width of about thirty yards, this being the length of the weir through which nearly the whole volume of water has to pass when the sluices heading the Agra canal just above the weir are closed. The monster weighing 136 lbs., caught by Mr. Van Cortland was, I believe, caught in the white water of the rapid, or just below it in the full strength of the stream, and I have frequently seen a goonch take my spoon or minnow here as soon as it touched the water.

They lie very often with their backs just out of water, and are easily shot with a bullet. Mr. Kirkpatrick, with whom I have more than once fished at this place, and in whose company I hope to do so again before many days are over, can corroborate my experience on this point.

As regards the *Wallago attu*, shown in plate 17, it appears to be better known in Upper India among natives by the name of Mulley than by that of Bawalli; but the one word may be a corruption of the other. I have also generally heard the *murral* called the *saul*, and not the *Wallago attu*.

With reference to "Rod's" first letter in the *Asian* of the 13th instant, on the effects of temperature, I have generally found that in the cold season predatory fish do not take freely, at least in tanks.

My experience of river fishing in the cold season is very limited, and I have only noticed personally one exception to this, which occurred on the 17th, 18th, and 19th February last year. I fished on those dates in a tank in the Hissar district, from 1 P.M. until 4 P.M., and killed respectively eight, six, and one fish of the *Wallago attu* species, with a spoon as big as a dessert-spoon, silver plated on both sides.

These fish ran from 3 lbs. to 15 lbs., average weight 6½ lbs.

I had in the month of June in the preceding year killed 125 of these fish in three days, with spoon and minnow, but they only averaged 3 lbs., as the tank was very much overstocked with them, and they were probably half starved. This thinning out of them evidently improved their size very rapidly, as only eight months elapsed between the two occasions, and it evidently shows that these fish grow at a most astounding rate when able to obtain plenty of food.

The days in February above quoted were bitterly cold, especially the 17th, on which I killed eight fish,—in fact so cold (after heavy rain a day or two before) that, although I had shot on foot along a ten-mile stage, from 8-30 A.M. until midday, I was shivering when I arrived at my camp.

I do not think, however, that the habits of predatory fish in tanks afford anything like an accurate test of the same fish in rivers.

On the 11th of this month I fished at Okhla in a cold wind but a hot sun, and did not rise a fish, though I saw a few (all of predaceous species) rising at about 3-30 P.M., and the belief is general, as far as I can discover, among fishermen in the Panjab, that the cold season is not suitable for fishing, even when the water is in good order, as it generally is at that season, in this part of India.

YUBA BILL.

DELHI, 22*nd February* 1883.

For descriptive formula, please see Chapter VIII.

Though not precisely pertaining perhaps to this chapter, which is headed "Live-bait picketing" I may conveniently introduce here that dead-bait picketed at the bottom, say a night line, will take Eels. The true eel is *Anguila Bengalensis*, for further particulars of which please find him at the close of Chapter VIII on the names and distribution of fish to be taken with a rod and line. *Mastacemblus armatus*, also to be found in that chapter, and mentioned as *Kal-ārāl*, is, from an angler's point of view, practically an eel, with a tendril protruding from his nose.

The bait is a dead fish of 3 or 4 inches long, threaded with a baiting needle on an eel gorge hook, which is a double hook on twisted wire with lead on the shank. Pass the baiting needle in at the mouth, and out at the fork of the tail, pulling the wire of the hook after it loop foremost, till the lead lies in the belly of the bait and the hooks close up to its mouth. Throw it well out and let it lie at the bottom. No rod is necessary.

Requisites for a week's trip.

Rod.—Any large strong rod, stiff or pliable as you chance to have it. A 14 ft. double handed trout rod is not strong enough. I use my Mahseer or Salmon rods, you may equally use a bamboo if mounted with rings.

Winch.—3 inches in diameter. More if you like, not less; but that is enough.

Running Line.—120 yards of strong running line such as you would use for Mahseer, Salmon or Pike.

Sinker.—Any sinker weighing about an ounce. Take 3.

Hooks.—Three No. 1 eyed Limerick hooks. Six No. 5 treble hooks.

Wire.—Treble twisted annealed wire, 2 yards, (page 75).

Gaff Hook.—1 gaff hook screwing into a handle, or a make shift of a large sea hook lashed to a bamboo with the barb broken off.

CHAPTER III.

LIVE-BAIT WITH A FLOAT.

> Unless it be
> The fond credulity
> Of silly fish, which worldling-like still look
> Upon the bait, but never on the hook.
>
> IZAAK WALTON.

Marral.

I AM not much in love with Marral myself, they give so little play. However some are, and I suppose I am a spoilt child of Mahseer and Labeo, and I promised to show you how to put them into a piedish; and it should not be overlooked that it is one of the commonest fish in India. You find them in almost every pond you come across. The natives consider them one of the best eating freshwater fish, placing them next perhaps to the gudgeon, and as they are very tenacious of life, and able to endure long exposure to the air out of water, a little sprinkling of water being quite enough to moisten and keep them alive for hours, they are very portable, and lend themselves to easy transport. Consequently natives, Mussalmans in particular, are much given to introducing them into any water, even into wells. This tenacity of life also makes them keep fresh for the table, in fact they are not unfrequently still alive when they reach the cook. In Calcutta they may be seen any day in the fish market, and especially on Fridays, all alive on the slabs, the salesmen freshening them up with an occasional sprinkle of water.

I may mention the following incident illustrative of their tenacity of life out of water. A friend rode to my door one morning and full of interest assured me "There was a live

Plate IX

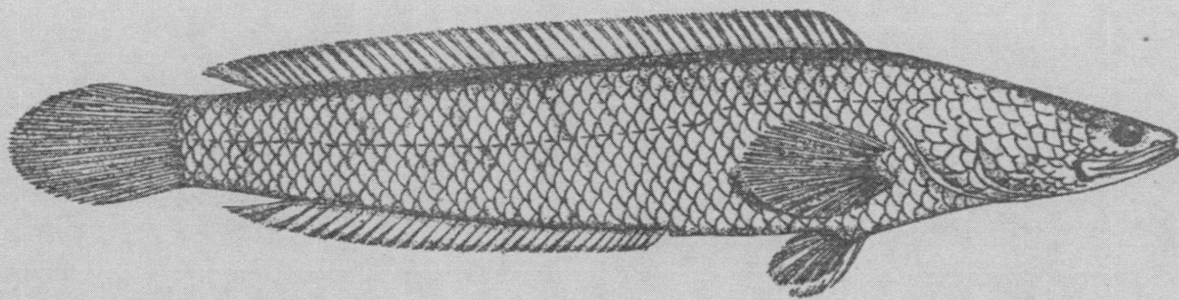

OPHIOCEPHALUS STRIATUS

"fish at the Club bar last night, ordering his whiskey and soda "for all the world as if he was a Club member. There was "indeed, and I have ordered him to be kept and sent to you." I thanked him and said I would tell him what fish it was when I saw it, but that I was pretty confident I could predicate that it was one of the *Ophiocephalidæ*, and most probably *Ophiocephalus gachua*. It turned out I was right. As I had surmised, the rain of the night in question, flowing from the Club roof, had made a very small certainly, but still a continuous connection from the Club, along the road, to the nearest road drain, and then by many road drains to the river, and up all these the fish had struggled more than half out of water till, on the stone pavement of the Club bar, he was quite out of water and flopped on at random, all alive and kicking still.

The best way of fishing for Marral is with a small live bait attached to a float, a good sized substantial cork float such as you would use in England when live baiting for perch or pike. Briefly it must be a float which your bait cannot take under water, but the Marral can. Use a No. 4 or 5 eyed Limerick hook with a small live bait of about 4½ inches long, tail included. Some prefer two No. 6 Limerick hooks tied back to back, or what answers the same purpose a double eel hook, on the ground that you are more likely to hook your Marral, and that, being attached to the bait by the back fin, it is not seen by the Marral, which ordinarily approaches from below your bait.

The size of the bait is a matter of much discussion, different anglers fancying different sizes from 3½ to 4½ inches long, tail included, and it is astonishing what a difference in size a single inch makes. The comparative advantages are briefly that the Marral prefers the larger sized bait of the two, but that at the same time the larger bait gives the angler more trouble by eternally running you into the weeds. But if it is catching the fish you sit there for, I suppose it is worth taking trouble. I would say then keep to the $4\frac{1}{2}$ inch bait. The larger bait, besides being more attractive, has the extra advantage of the better covering your double hook.

Fish near the surface, say 2 feet off it. About this there need be no doubt. You have only to look at the position of the eye in the Marral (*Ophiocephalus*) to see that they are placed for looking mainly upwards.

Strike when he takes you under or moves off in a way that must be beyond the powers of your bait. Shot or lead wire your line to keep the bait down. You will find 2 lbs. to be the average size of the Marral you will take, though they do run much larger, and you may occasionally, indeed not infrequently get them 2 and 3 feet long. They are very shy, and you will be careful to keep well out of sight. It is mainly on account of their shyness that they are better taken with a live bait than spinning, though I have taken them both ways.

As I am not sufficiently keen about Marral myself I can best infuse a little enthusiasm into my page by quoting from one who is. He writes me "I have had a red letter day "to-day; 9 Marral weighing 14 lbs.; six of them 2 lbs. "each, one 1 lb., and two half a pound each. H, who was "fishing with me, got 6 lbs. making just 20 lbs. between us. "The day before yesterday H got 4 weighing $7\frac{1}{2}$ lbs. and a "day or two before I got 5 weighing a little over 7 lbs. "together." * * "We fished with live bait on single "gut." * * "We caught some turtles too."

Marral have teeth like a Pike, in fact you may call them the Indian Pike; consequently it is quite on the cards they may bite through your gut. But risk it and you'll have more bites than if you use too obvious gimp. Possibly my treble wire may prove a good compromise; but I have not tried it, and B and H above always fish with gut in spite of the teeth. I too have caught Marral on gut and not been cut. On the other hand I have also been cut, when playing a good one, and he has had more time to consider the position.

There it is then, it is for you to decide. Will you run the risk of losing a good one now and then in the prospect of getting more bites and more fun on the whole, or do you believe in "the simplicity of the 3 per cents." as an investment? If the latter use thin wire, if the former gut. I would incline to happy-go-lucky being the better dog, because after all it is not so very much that you lose if you are cut, and it is more than even betting in your favor. It is not like a mighty Mahseer disappearing with a monstrous swirl that leaves you unconsoleably sorrowing for the rest of your miserable existence. There the game is worth making sure of; here you may as well do a little playful speculating.

A writer in "*The Asian*" says he has had excellent fly fishing for Marral. He was kind enough to send me his fly. It was a very full thickly dressed Black-palmer on a No. 5 Limerick hook.

Marral may also be taken by dapping with a live frog, stiff rod, and strong tackle. Dap on to the leaf of a water lily. It is like a knock at the door to tell the Marral you are coming in. Then dap between the lilies and if you are taken lift your friend straight out without ceremony.

You may also set a line hanging from a fixed rod point, or from an overhanging bough so that a live frog shall sit naturally on the top of the water. This is the Asiatic Trimmer set forth at greater length with other matter about the Marral in "*The Rod in India*."

For descriptive formula about the Marral or *Ophiocephalus* the reader is referred to Chapter VIII.

Requisites for a week's fishing.

ROD, WINCH, RUNNING-LINE.—The same as used for Labeo will do for live bait fishing. If you *also* want tackle for dapping among lilies have a stiff strong pike rod and pike running line; but it is not a necessary, the live bait fishing being the best (page 70).

HOOKS.—Six No. 4 eyed Limerick hooks bare.
GUT.—Twelve lengths thin Salmon gut.
FLOAT.—A large cork float.
SINKER.—Two yards soft lead wire to put on your gut in place of split shot, or a make shift of the tin foil in which tea is wrapped.

Puftahs.

The same style of fishing seems to suit the Puftah. This is a fish I have not caught myself, so I warn you the following is only hearsay. Still I have it on good testimony and the fishing seems too good to omit on the sole ground of the knowledge not being personal; so I give it you as I have heard it.

They are not infrequently to be found in river-fed ponds such as have been mentioned as containing Labeo and Fresh-water Shark. They run from $2\frac{1}{2}$ to 5 lbs. says my authority. He never caught one under $2\frac{1}{2}$ lbs. Still I do not suppose he wishes us to believe they are born that size! Another fisherman has caught them up to 6 and 7 lbs., and I dare say another might catch them under $2\frac{1}{2}$ lbs. if he used a worm instead of a small fish as bait. Both assure me they, i.e. the fish not the assurers, are very game and active, and on other hands also I hear that Puftahs are well worth fishing for.

They are very wary, so you cannot use gimp but a fine wire. It seems you cannot risk gut as with the Marral, their teeth being worse. Use a No. 6 Limerick hook and fish at one-quarter of the depth of the water with a small 2 inch bait as above suggested for Marral.

Puftah seems to be the Hindustani name for *Callichrous bimaculatus* for which the Tamil is *Kellati*. But I am only going by hearsay I am sorry to say. I have not seen a specimen to identify personally. I must apologize most humbly for mentioning at all a fish of which I know so little personally. I am driven to make some sort of mention of it by the keen-

Plate X

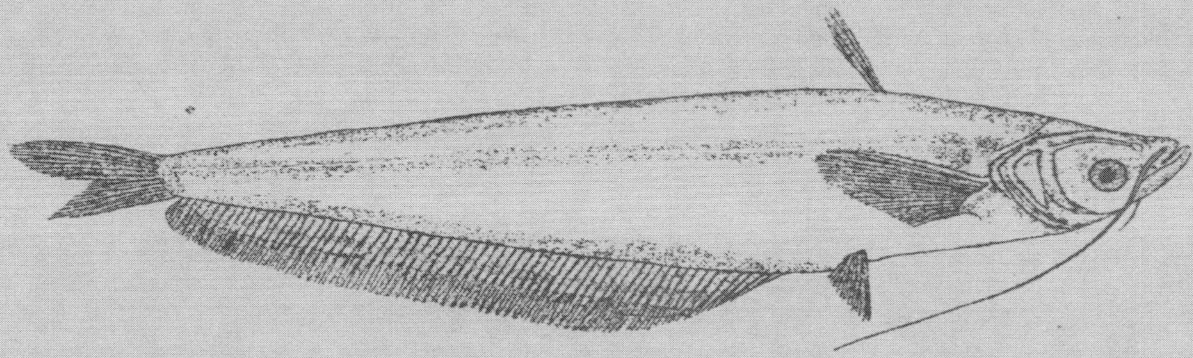

CALLICHROUS BIMACULATUS

Plate XI

NOTOPTERUS CHITALA

Plate XII

NOTOPTERUS KAPIRAT

Plate XIII

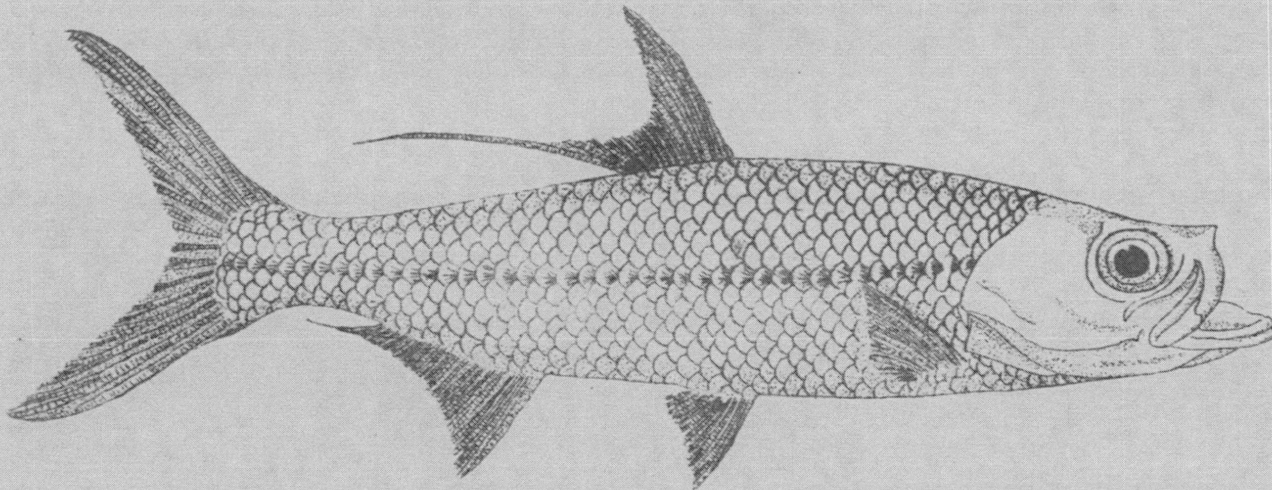

MEGALOPS CYPRINOIDES

ness with which my informant spoke of it, and in the hope that between us we may make something of this fish by the time we come to another edition. This mention is only provocative, more than enough so I fear.

The Siluroid family is a large one and a predaceous one; it is probable therefore that all the minor branches thereof may be taken in this way, and the major ones in the manner suggested for *Wallago attu*, our Freshwater Shark. These two systems should therefore embrace well nigh all the predaceous fish of India.

Notopterus chitala.

Notopterus Chitala, the *Chitala* or *Setal* of Northern India and Assam, which runs to 4 ft. long, and is a deep flat-sided fish, may, I hear, be taken in the same way as Marral and Puftah. So may the larger ones of the *Notopterus kapirat* of Southern India, which do not seem to run over 2 lbs. while the smaller ones are best taken with a worm or prawn.

Megalops cyprinoides.

Megalops cyprinoides, the big-eye, mentioned in *The Rod in India*, *Morāng kendai* of Tamil, an estuary fish frequently acclimatized to freshwater in ponds, may also be taken in the same way. So may *Elops saurus*, *Ālāti* of Tamil, in Estuaries. Small Freshwater Shark will also take the small live-bait meant for Marral.

For descriptive formula of all these fish, please see Chapter VIII.

Requisites for a week's fishing.—The same as for live-bait fishing for Marral (page 85).

CHAPTER IV.

WORM AND PRAWN FISHING.

I wish you all joy of the worm.

ANTONY AND CLEOPATRA.

A No. 6 Limerick hook on gut with a worm and a light float will catch several sorts of fish. Fish on the bottom. A dead prawn will prove even more attractive. Always shell your prawn; fish prefer them served so. I have known Labeo of 3 and 4 lbs., and Freshwater Shark of 1 and 2 lbs. taken on a worm resting on the bottom. Indeed there are few fish that despise a worm, so that a worm-fisher's bag is likely to be a varied one. Turtles prefer worm to paste.

The native method of scouring a worm is very simple. They put their worms in fine gravel or red earth, and the change produced is certainly a very rapid one. When you cannot get moss you may transfer them from the gravelly soil, after a ten minutes' course thereof, to fine grass pressed tightly together. Still leaving them in the gravelly soil will not injure them.

Gudgeon.

The Indian Gudgeon, *Gobius giuris,* called trisyllabically *Ulave* in Tamil, and mud fish in Calcutta, and attaining a foot and a half in length, and 3 lbs. in weight, may be taken with a worm or a prawn in ponds. It is a bold biter, has a wide gaping mouth full of fine teeth, and will take your float well under and away. Strike when it does. It is a yellowish very transparent fish with a singularly flat and big head. It is much esteemed by natives as the best of tank fish for eating, and you have a recipe above for cooking it.

Plate XIV

GOBIUS GIURIS

Notopterus kapirat.

Notopterus kapirat, the *Chotta-vāle* of Tamil, a flat-sided deep silvery fish with a small head and mouth, not exceeding 2 lbs., and more ordinarily running half and three-quarters of a pound, may be taken with a worm, or a dead prawn, the latter for preference, on a No. 6 or 8 Limerick hook, the former for prawn, the latter for worm. Strike either when he runs away with your float, or, if he turns canny, when the float bobs vigorously. Use the detective float (page 23).

I have killed these fish and I think it is a simple business, and that the above is enough to say about them. But I must admit I am not so keen over them as *Fleur de Lys* is, perhaps because I have not fished so often for them and do not know as much about them. For the benefit of my readers therefore I will take the liberty to extract the following from his letter to *The Asian* of 14th June 1887:—

* * * * * *

The mouth of the Notopterus is very tender, and you require a light hand, or you will lose numbers in the landing. If the fish are biting shyly you hook nearly all of them by the very edge of their lip, and the least roughness breaks away your hook-hold at once. No exact rule can be laid down as to the best size of hook; it entirely depends on the humour the fish are in. If the water is heavy, and they are biting boldly, a No. 6 or No. 7 Limerick (Thomas' scale) is as good as any; but if the water is fine and the fish are shy, I recommend a No. 9 or No. 10 Sneck hook *wrapped with white silk*, for on this small hook you can present one of those tiny, tasty, red worms that the souls of fish delight in. The Sneck hooks are so thin and delicate that it is easier to thread a small worm on them than on other hooks, and you can make a neater job of it.

The Notopterus takes a worm better than anything else; now and then they take a prawn well, and I have even caught a large one on a live-bait. You should always plumb the depth most carefully in bottom fishing and have your worm just resting on the ground. Ground baiting beforehand improves the fishing greatly, and a few loose worms thrown in now and then *while you are fishing* will collect the fish together.

* * * * * *

The bite of the Notopterus is recognizable from that of other fish, although it is very hard to describe in what the difference lies. When these fish are in a shy mood it will take you all you know to catch them; the float will shake gently for about half a minute and then your friend will retire having successfully bitten the tail of the worm off and exposed the point of the hook. Next time you will probably nail him if you put on a small tasty worm with very little *loose end*, or if you gain his confidence by throwing in half a dozen worms for him to tuck into while you fish for five minutes in another place. All these little episodes help to give a charm to bottom fishing, and it is a little feather in your cap to remember how you at last got round some wary old stager after he had eaten half a pot of your worms!

* * * * * *

Notopterus take best in the early morning and evening, but during the cold weather just after the rains they take well all day.

I confess I do not see the point of the white silk wrapping, for you are going to hide it with a worm, and if it is not well covered a less attractive color would be preferable.

Etroplus Suratensis.

Etroplus Suratensis, known in Tamil as *Panni-kendai*, is a small deep rather flat-sided fish, something like a bream in shape, with prominent nibbling teeth with which it feeds largely on vegetables, and will pull up every bit of weed in an aquarium. The natives ordinarily fish for it with thread weed (in Tamil *nūl pāshi* or *pacha pāshi*) wound round and round the hook, and fish at a foot and a half from the surface. But I have seen it successfully taken, and taken it myself, with a fine worm on the bottom. Those in my aquarium take a large worm also, and have a curious way of very soon ejecting its cuticle, having somehow treated it just as an ordinary school boy does a fresh gooseberry. Still the mouth is small, and the most successful way of fishing seems to be with a fine worm on a No. 10 Limerick hook or other hook of that size on fine gut, with a sensitive float, say a detective float of 3 or 4 inches long instead of 6 inches in length and a good deal thinner and lighter than the ordinary detective float. Do not use an eyed hook because the fine worm will not run up it. He is a subtle biter. Strike when he bobs freely and vigorously; *Fleur de Lys* writes me that at times when they are

Plate XV

ETROPLUS SURATENSIS

wary you must also strike for a mere quiver, as we do for Labeo. It is not safe to wait till he runs away with your float, though he will do that too sometimes.

He is a very pretty greenish fish, crossed with several bars and white spotted all over. He runs to 2 lbs. and makes a very free fight for his size, and will break your very light tackle for you if you are not careful. Use a very light little rod for quick striking. There is nothing better than the native sprig of bamboo set in a reed handle of what they call false sugar cane, literally devil's sugar cane, *pē-kărămbu* in Tamil, and in all 9 ft. in length. Value about 2 annas.

This fish seems to frequent the neighbourhood of the Coast only, though it is a freshwater fish accommodating itself to brackish water. I do not remember seeing it in ponds. It is plentiful in the Fort ditch at Madras, which is somewhat brackish, and in the Adyar, above the Farm anicut, which is sweet, and I do not see why it should not be bred in ponds for home fishing.

I learnt this fishing from *Fleur de Lys* so I will quote him on it.

Another fish which is to be caught with the same tackle and bait as the *Notopterus* is the *Etroplus Suratensis*, though they usually do not frequent the same water. * * * * * For this fish there is no better hook than the Sneck bend No. 10 (Thomas' scale); it should be wrapped to fine gut. The Etroplus is a weed-feeder, but takes a small red worm freely; it is a much more accomplished bait-stealer than the Notopterus, but the lips are tough and leathery and afford a good hook-hold. It is a very powerful fish for its size, and a pound fish on fine gut will take you all you know to land it. Etroplus greatly effect the shallows of a tank or river and congregate near rocks and stones, and if there are wooden palings going into the water, they are often to be found round about them, probably for the sake of the moss and weeds. In a tank I used to fish, one of the best places was round some railings which ran into the water, as I have described, and many a fish have I lost, through its bolting through the rails and cutting my gut line. I have seen an Etroplus two pounds in weight, and I have no doubt that they grow even larger. A half pound fish gives you plenty of fun, their peculiar platelike form giving them great power in the water. The mouth is so tiny that a larger hook than No. 10 Sneck is almost useless; the worm must be very neatly put on or the Etroplus will not look at it. * * * I have caught as many as two and three dozen of an evening. Two dozen fish, as a rule, will weigh together from 4½ to 5 lbs., as six to the pound is the commonest size for these fish.

On hot days the Etroplus may be seen basking in large shoals on the surface. They take best from about five o'clock until dusk; the larger fish especially seem very particular as to the time of day they feed. I recollect seeing two Etroplus, of half a pound a piece once in some shallow water. I tried them with the most tempting worms, but they would take no notice, so I went on fishing in another place. Just before dusk I thought I would try these two fish again, and no sooner had I dropped a worm in front of them, than the larger took it. I got him out, and dropped another worm in front of the second one, which had not stirred from the place, and got that one too; so that these two fish were apparently waiting until dinner time, and would look at nothing between meals! Catch the Etroplus but don't try and eat him; he is one of the nastiest fish on record.

On the contrary another friend assures me they are excellent eating. I have never tried myself, but hazard the surmise that both my friends are right, *Fleur de Lys* having caught his fish in the Madras Fort moat, which is freely sewer-fed, and my other friend having caught his in clean water.

It is astonishing what fish people will catch. I am sure there are not a few who are of the same mind as the gentleman who had the courage to say he would rather catch tadpoles than catch nothing. I remember seeing two rods eagerly fishing for *Etroplus maculatus*, and one being pointed out to me as the expert thereat. *Etroplus maculatus* is little cousin to *E. Suratensis* having a brilliant gambouge stomach, and a black spot on its side, breeds freely in ponds, and takes a worm; but it is only fit to transfer to a small globe aquarium, in which it is a very pretty object.

I believe I am fairly keen when fish worth catching are in question, indeed I am half voted a nuisance in camp for rout-

Plate XVI

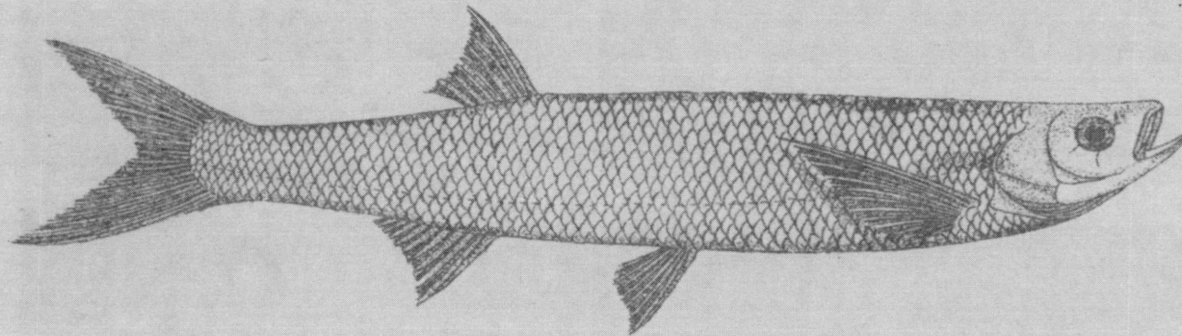

CHELA ARGENTEA

ing men out "so early in the morning," and when, breakfast being swallowed, I said "Come on D——, let's get at them again," the solemn awe-striking charge of a lazy comfortably-digesting one was, "You'll *kill* D——." But D—— came along like a broth-of-a-boy, and isn't dead yet. Still it was Mahseer and Carnatic Carp fishing we were then doing, and I am afraid my readers find me many degrees below par when we come to small fish that present no difficulty in the catching, and no weight on the line when you have hooked them. For lack of sufficient enthusiasm of my own I have already had to indent, in the matter of small fish, on the ardor of *Fleur de Lys* to spice my page, and now that we come to little two or three-inch urchins like *Etroplus maculatus*, my keenness is fairly played out, and I have nowhere to look for aid. And yet it was only today that one told me they were capital fun, and I must not omit them, and he had caught whole strings of them. The mad enthusiasm of such an one takes one back by a long leap to classic days. My classical readers will readily recall the incident, though where it was one read it I could not tell you now for the life of me. It was Keanest McKeanor was being ferried over the Styx, when he begged Charon to hold hard for a minute that he might have just one cast in a likely bit.

Chela argentia.

Chela of sorts are to be found in most ponds and tanks, and may be taken with a small dace fly, or with a grain of rice or any paste or worm on a No. 14 Sneck bend hook within a foot of the surface, using the tiniest float. Both for these and Etroplus the best float is a detective float half the length and half the thickness used for Labeo. If you ground bait for them you will readily get them round you in numbers. For this throw in dry bran all about your float. Being dry it will float and attract the Chela, which are surface-swimmers, better than if it sank. Fried rice is commonly sold in the bazaar. It is white, and very buoyant, and if pounded makes a still better surface bait than bran.

Chela are generally considered a good bait for Mahseer and Freshwater Shark and so they are while they last. But they are a very delicate fish, dying soon as live bait, and coming to pieces soon as dead bait. Therefore though they are frequently the most easily caught and the most tempting bait, they are to my mind more trouble than they are worth, and I prefer a small carp of a tougher sort.

They are said to behave well in a dish, but except from hearsay I know nothing.

For descriptive details of all the fish mentioned in this chapter I must refer the reader, as heretofore, to Chapter VIII. The notices being each so short it hardly seems necessary to summarise the fishing requisites.

CHAPTER V.

LOCALITIES.

> May pure contents
> For ever pitch their tents
> Upon these downs, these meads, these rocks, these mountains
> And peace still slumber by these purling fountains
> Which we may every year
> Meet, when we come a-fishing here.
>
> IZAAK WALTON.

THE localities suitable for tank fishing are of the nature described on page 13. How to do more than tell you this is not easy, as I know so few places as yet, and of these some are private property, to fish in which leave has been obtained as a personal favor, and it scarcely seems a fair return for such favors to publish them to all the world. It is not that I desire to keep these places dark to myself. In all my fishing I have never done that. My principle has always been to tell out everything at once so as to help others to sport, and many a day have I given up my own rod to lay a brother angler in. Still I must not forget what is due to parties who have made personal exceptions in my favor, and with only the reservation that I am bound to make on account of these obligations I will do all I fairly can to direct my readers to good localities; in the hope that fishermen will return the compliment by telling me of other places, especially places near the Presidency Towns, so that a run out and back can easily be made on a short holiday. If they will they may be sure that in the next edition they will get in the aggregate a great deal more than any one can give individually, for I cannot but think that such places must be numerous, and as

I shall indicate hereafter their number might be still further enlarged.

MADRAS DISTRICT.

The Red Hill Lake is seven miles from Madras, so that one can drive out in the morning and come back the same evening. It contains Labeo, Freshwater Shark, and Olive Carp to my knowledge, besides Chela and other minor fish, and probably many others. It is I understand never netted, and rightly so, because netting would disturb the bottom, and befoul the drinking supply of the Presidency town. But rod fishing could not do any manner of harm. One objection is that it is best fished from a boat in the deep water near the islands, and a boat is a matter of favor. Natives fish commonly from the embankment which is near the surplusage and furthest from the Madras supply channel. But I have never seen them catch Labeo there, only the minor carp of sorts. I imagine it is because they do not get out into the deep water. The great objection is, and it is a serious one, that such a large unsheltered piece of water is wind-swept, and then the waves are such that your float is in constant motion, and you cannot possibly detect the subtle bite of the Labeo. Still there are quiet days, if one only knew them, and capital bags have been made there from a boat.

The Ponds in the People's Park, Madras, hold Marral, *Notopterus kapirat*, Indian Gudgeon, Freshwater Shark, *Megalops cyprinoides*, *Chanos salmoneus*, and may be others that I know not of, besides, on Irish testimony, "Eels you could fly a kite with." There is a fishing charge.

The Madras Fort moat holds *Etroplus Suratensis*, besides the following fish mentioned in "*The Rod in India.*" *Lates calcarifer*, *Megalops cyprinoides*, *Elops saurus*, *Lutianus roseus*, and I believe others. It holds also an unlimited quantity of Fort drainage matter, giving off a very fair amount of typhoid fever. It is too filthy for gentlemanly sport. *Odi et arceo.*

When flushed with flood waters in the rainy season I am told it is sweet and fishable for a time.

The dammed up waters of the Adyar at the Sydapet Farm hold to my knowledge Freshwater Shark, Labeo, Olive Carp, *Chela argentia*, *Etroplus Suratensis*, *Cirrhina reba*, and turtle, and if I remember rightly, *Megalops cyprinoides*. But they have been fished and netted to death, and I have never done any good there. It might make a fair preserve handy to Madrassees.

The pond behind The Women-and-Children's Hospital, between the Cooum and The Scotch Kirk holds Labeo, Olive Carp, Notopterus, Marral and black-bellied turtle, and may be more sorts not known to me for certain.

The pond behind The Mess House of the 3rd Regiment has been kindly thrown open to the members of *The Rod in India Club* by the Officers. The sepoys tell me it holds Freshwater Shark, Marral, Gudgeon, and Labeo.

It is proposed to well stock these two last-named ponds with Labeo and White Carp, and strictly preserve them.

TRICHINOPOLY DISTRICT.

At the Upper Anicut near Trichinopoly are Freshwater Shark and Puftahs, and may be others not within my knowledge. A kindly pen makes good my personal deficiencies in knowledge of this locality. Would I had more such communications.

I have not made the acquaintance of that gentleman the Mahseer, and should like to, but I am a believer in his non-existence in the district, and content myself with smaller fry in whose company I have been very happy.

The tanks set apart for bathing and drinking purposes within Municipal limits in the native town of Trichinopoly are fed by small channels from the Cāvēry, and are well stocked with fish, notably the Labeo, Freshwater Shark, and Keliti (Cat fish). I have taken some good specimens of them weighing I should say from 6 to 7 lbs. with paste made of rice flour cakes ("Iteli") ground up with curds and parched Bengal gram, and scented with toasted salt fish. The stone steps leading down to the water is where they take best, and I adjust my float with a plumb to the depth of about 2½ or 3 feet, and let the paste touch the stone steps at about that depth as lightly as possible. You can tell whether it does or not by your float, which if correctly adjusted should be about an inch or so out of water, and stand suspended in it obliquely. One not accustomed to this sort of fishing expects a grab and a rush, but watch your float and strike the moment it disappears under water after a few slight but quick bobs. Broiled rice bran mixed with cowdung answers very well as a ground bait to attract them to the steps.

The best tanks in Trichinopoly town are those known as the Banbury Teppucolam near the Municipal market, the Waraiyur Agrahram Teppucolam behind the S. P. G. Mission School at Waraiyur, and the Singāratope Teppucolam near the Fort gate. One has to provide himself with a pass from the Municipal Commissioner of the Division before he is allowed to fish in any of these tanks. It (the permit) holds good for 12 months and is procurable on payment of a fee of a rupee. The rules might be made more stringent, but as they exist at present, the holder of a permit may I believe give his friends chances of sport in any of the tanks for the rupee that he pays.

Then there is the Agrahram Teppucolam at Nangapuram which is also river-fed, and within easy distance (2 miles) of Elemanur Railway Station on the Erode line. The distance by rail from Trichinopoly to Elemanur being only 11 miles, and the train leaving the former station at 6, and arriving at the latter at about 7 A.M. I have frequently ridden across and spent a very pleasant morning at the tank before breakfast. The Forest Officers' Bungalow on the bank of the Cāvēry about 300 yards from Elemanur Railway Station, or the Engineers' and Collector's Bungalows at the Anicut are always available. The two first mentioned are not furnished, and it will be necessary to take out all you require.

Talking of the Anicut reminds me of the lampreys (*Ārāl*) to be had there. To be able to get at them you want a good sinker to your line so as to take your hook down to them between the stones below the Anicut where they are usually found. They are greedy fish, and enjoy a bit of earthworm immensely, and that seems to be about the best bait possible to keep on the hook, as to attract them you have to dangle it about their very noses and hook them out. Don't despise them because they wriggle so. They run to about 3 feet I believe, and if ever you hook a full-grown one in water clear of rocks and weeds, you will find him equal to his neighbours in affording you sport. Try in the tanks I have mentioned above, and you will find that they enjoy a bit of paste under a float, as well as they do a bit of earthworm in their hiding places between rocks.

Now a word about *Chela argentea* (silver fish). If you have a desire to cultivate their acquaintance, go to Tirvalarai, a village 14 miles north of Trichinopoly on the road to Turaiyur. They never seem to be very particular, and take fly, paste, earthworm, or in fact anything you may offer them. There is a good road from Trichinopoly almost to the tank I speak of, but you must be prepared for a bad camping ground, and trouble about provisions if you start badly supplied.

MADURA DISTRICT.

The best tank for Murrel is that at Shivagunga about 26 miles (if my memory serves me right) east of Madura on the road to Ramnad. The water is seldom or never clear of weeds, and I have shot some measuring quite 18 inches I should think, though I won't be quite sure not having measured and kept notes. Shot have no effect, you want something heavier, and can turn them over beautifully with a rook rifle as they come up among the weeds.

SALEM DISTRICT.

In answer to the enquiry on page 292 of *The Rod in India* as to whether fish sleep, I am inclined to say that they do. At all events, the "Uluvei" in the tank at the foot of the rock at Namcul in Salem District seem to, for I have seen them lounging on the stone steps in about an inch or so of water at noon, apparently unconscious of danger, allowing themselves to be taken with a horse hair noose tied at the end of a thin bamboo rod. Very stupid of them I thought.

GENERAL.

Fish have been found alive under sand in the bed of the Sattur river in Tinnevelly District while the bridge was under construction, and "Murrel" and "Uluvei" of sizes which I should say they could not have attained in a year, or even 18 months' time, have been found in a rain-fed tank at Kaligudi 16 miles north of Trichinopoly. The tank is dry about 3 months in the year, and I could not understand it at the time, but I do now.

I mention the "*Panai ēri Kendei" here as so little seems to be known about them. The tamil name would imply that they are a species of Carp fond of amusing themselves by climbing Palmyra trees for a change, though I must confess to not having seen them accomplish such extraordinary feats yet. They are pond fish running up to about 4 inches, and seem peculiar only to Karambadi near Negapatam.

* *Anabas scandens.*—Emerson Tennant's Natural History of Ceylon has a picture of one climbing a palmyra.

TINNEVELLY DISTRICT.

There is good fishing to be had at the Streevignntam Anicut I am told, but I have never had the chance of trying. Being so near the sea there is no reason why there should not be any Hilsa about during the season. The Anicut is about 14 miles east of Palamcotta, and there is a good camping ground near it.

Eels.

The natives have an easy way of taking them. They leave small-mouthed earthen pots with a bit of sheep skin in each over night, and draw them up in the morning with their fish lying coiled up most comfortably in them.

The writer of the above paper is quite correct in saying that if you strike when he tells you you will get fish; but I may be allowed to add that if you never strike for anything less you will miss many a good fish. One is naturally inclined to think that anything less than he mentions is merely the nibble of provokingly small fish, but, as stated above, the best fish bite most subtilely, and many a first class Labeo may be taken on the merest quiver. The nibbling of small fry is distinct, and you will get to distinguish it. Again and again we have had small fry at us the moment our float had settled, and we bemoaned our misfortune, but presently the nibbling ceased, and was succeeded by more cautious biting, which we recognized at once as being that of a Labeo. The history of it probably was that the small fry being busy round the bait served to give the Labeo a hint that they had found something, and he thereon warned them off, and took it himself. How these small fry do annoy one. It is some satisfaction to think that they too are annoyed in turn by being unceremoniously hustled whenever they are seen commencing their dinner. They are the lion's jackals.

The writer speaks of fishing on the steps. We too commenced by doing the same. Herein we followed the native fishermen. The idea is that it is there the fish congregate, and there only that you can get a reliably flat bottom for the exact regulation of your float. But we have since found that more and bigger fish may be caught away from the steps if you can only find a piece of even bottom, and will have a little patience ground-baiting it.

The writer's lampreys, *Ārāl* in Tamil, are doubtless *Mastacemblus armatus.* It has not the sucker mouth of the lamprey placed underneath the snout, and it does not go to sea. It is more like an eel, with a protruding tendril on its snout, and a row of spines along the back. We have taken it on dead fish on a night line. It has a little chapter to itself in "*The Rod in India*" and a few words above, and you may also give it a pie-dish to itself with advantage, cooking it according to the recipe for Eels. I am not aware that there is such a thing as a lamprey in India. So in India you are safe from dying, like the English King, from overeating them.

TANJORE DISTRICT.

Take the road from Tanjore to Combaconum and after driving about 5 miles take the road branching to your left, and after about another half mile or mile you will find a pond on your left by the road side, and a little further on a built tank in a private compound to your right. In both of these are Labeo, White Carp and Freshwater Shark in plenty. For the second tank you will require to seek the permission of the owner.

There is a pond attached to a small temple in the Vadakudi village half a mile off the road, at a point about a mile from Negapatam on the Karekal road where there is a road-side Chattram on the inland side of the road. The bye-way goes between the Chattram and a pond. The pond half a mile on is well stocked with Labeo, Freshwater Shark and Puftahs. It is private property and is never netted. Permission for rod fishing is obtainable on previous application. There is a tank near a Chattram about a mile out of Combaconum which might give good sport if they did not net it. Negapatam town has good river-fed tanks in it, which would give excellent sport if not rented out for netting, and if sanitarily treated as the Trichinopoly tanks are.

At Manărgudi, nine miles by good road from Nidamangalam Railway station and covered by a constant service of rapid little vehicles called jutkas, is a tank called the Rukamani tank, covering about an acre well stocked with Labeo, White Carp, Olive Carp, and other fish. They do not run over 3 lbs. as yet, having had only 2 years' immunity from netting, but they are very plentiful. As the exclusive fishing of this tank has been rented for a term of years by *The Rod in India Club* and it will be strictly preserved in future, the fishing in it should very shortly be beyond praise.

In the same town of Manărgudi is a magnificent built square tank each side of which is a quarter of a mile in length; and the depth in the dry and wet weather varies from 9 ft. to 15 ft. they say. It used to swarm with fish, running some of them to 20 lbs. But it has been fished and netted to death. Two friends and self spent half a day on it without a bite and had to give it up as a bad job. But what a magnificent fishery it might make if sanitarily kept from the net. There is a river close by from which 10,000 fry a year of good sorts could easily be put in at 8 annas a thousand.

BELLARY DISTRICT.

A good sportsman writes me that in the larger tanks such as Darojee he used to catch a lot of Puftahs.

BURMAH.

I have ample testimony of huge Labeo and monster Freshwater Sharks being caught in the moat at Mandalay.

CALCUTTA.

The ponds in the Zoological Gardens, Calcutta hold Catla, Labeo, Mirgha, and probably other fish; besides prawns without number.

The Havildar's tank and other ponds on the maidan hold Catla, Labeo, Mirgha, Indian Gudgeon, Sărăl-poti, Megalops, and may be others.

CHAPTER VI.

STOCKING PONDS.

THE opportunities for stocking ponds in Calcutta are far in advance of anything obtaining in Southern India, because the natives there are in the habit of annually stocking their ponds with fry caught from the rivers. This they do for the purpose of netting their stews and eating the fish when grown. A wealthy and intelligent native there explained to me that they were their cutlets, their crumb-chops, their beef-steaks, &c., &c., &c. The fishermen therefore are habituated to dealing with fry of the more valuable sorts, they know how to catch them and what is much more to the point, how to carry them without loss from overcrowding. In the Madras Presidency on the contrary no amount of talking will knock it into the heads of the fishermen that you cannot overcrowd fish with impunity. In Calcutta however the regular annual demand has created a regular supply and induced intelligent treatment. The consequence is that you can readily buy at known prices any of the valuable sorts you like to specify, and you will have no difficulty, for it is an established trade, in getting the fry of the sorts you want and no others. The rapidity with which the practised eye of a professional fisherman picks out of a lot the particular fry desired is worth looking at. They do it unerringly as quick as a cashkeeper separates copper from silver coins. If therefore Calcutta anglers are bitten by the remarks I have offered on tank fishing there is no reason why they should not knock us altogether into a cocked hat, for their tank fish, as well as their facilities, are very much finer than ours. Our little bag of 678 lbs. to 4 rods in 3 days should be small by what they ought to be able to achieve. We have no Catlas running to 50 and 100 lbs. Our *Cirrhina cirrhosa* is smaller than their 18-lb. *Cirrhina mrigala* (*Mirga*), and they equal us in Rohi, Kalabous and other Labeo. There is no reason therefore why they should not annually turn into their ponds in thousands fry of the following sorts. Mirgha, and Rohi above all others for preference now that we well know how to catch them. Kalabous and Catla may be added. Make a rule that every fish of these sorts under a foot in length is to be returned to the water immediately, and time will work the rest for you. The restriction should not extend to the Gudgeon and other smaller sorts already in the ponds. The more of them that are taken out of the ponds the better for the fry to be turned in, for the Indian Gudgeon is a sad fry eater. The Catla too is said to do a little business that way, as all Carps do that grow to any great size, notably the Mahseer.

In the Madras Presidency also much might be done in the way of stocking ponds if only there was a demand for fry which would induce the fishermen to learn how to carry them alive intelligently: or if any Association of Anglers would take it in hand to supervise them by an intelligent agent, and, buying fry from them, stock ponds preserved for rod fishing.

Trichinopoly has set an intelligent example that might well be followed in all Municipalities with sanitary advantage. Ordinarily the practice is for Municipalities to let out to a contractor the netting of their ponds for an annual Rs. 20 or Rs. 30; and the consequence is that when they are at the lowest at the close of the dry season the ponds are netted to death, nothing the size of a tadpole being suffered to survive. But in Trichinopoly it is intelligently recognized that to allow netting in tanks used by the Municipal tax-payers for bathing, drinking, and cooking purposes, is to stir up the bottom and befoul the water to the inconvenience of the bathers, and to the sanitary injury of the drinkers of the thus disturbed water; and that it is worth a great deal more than Rs. 20 or Rs. 30 to the tax-payers to have their water-supply undisturbed. The owner of a large tank that was much used by the towns-people went still further, and said that the fish in the tank purified the water, which they doubtless do by assimilating impurities. Recognizing this, Trichinopoly allows no netting, but permits rod fishing on payment of a charge. If all Municipalities had the sense to do this they would certainly find their advantage sanitarily, and whether or not they did so financially also by rod licences is, considering the amount at stake, and the health of the people, a very secondary question. An Anglers' Association might well settle this question for them by taking up certain of these tanks for a consideration, and reserving them for the angling of members. A few such tanks within easy reach of Madras would be very acceptable. Since these lines were written *The Rod in India Club* has been formed, and is undertaking it. What more it may do for the improvement of river-fishing also and of fishing at the Hill Sanitaria is presumedly a question of funds.

The tanks in point are spontaneously fed with fry through the channels in connection with a river. In the freshes the fry, following their migratory instinct, come in as little things weighing a drachm or so, and grow in the tanks to 6, 8 and even 20 lbs.

From the variableness of rivers in tropical India the fish are of necessity much more migratory than in Europe. Carp that would be stationary in Europe are in India highly migratory. This has been dwelt on at length in "*The Rod in India.*" This intensified migratory tendency is largely taken advantage of to capture them in fixed engines, and such fixed engines, used now only for destruction of fry, might equally be used for the preservation of the better species. If I quote from a paper of my own written in reply to one from the President of the Punjab Angling Club, it may serve to illustrate how the tanks in point could be further supplied with valuable sorts of fish, and how other tanks also which are not river-fed could be stocked, if the fry had not to be carried any expensive distance.

"The experience of my last Christmas holiday outing, small as it is, seems to me, sufficiently illustrative of the value of fishery protection. Near our fishing place was an irrigation channel, across which was constructed a close meshed cruive. Looking at the fish taken in it I observed that they weighed each a few drachms at most, and I heard and saw that a double handful of them was sold for one-twelfth of an anna, and yet not a few of these miserable morsels were fry of fish that ran to 20 lbs. each. Seeing such things is believing, but how to reproduce them for the conviction of other minds is more difficult. I wanted to do so, as I have wanted any time this last 17 years. So I told the owner of the cruive that I would buy a pot-full of him, and in four hours he brought me a large potful. With my two friends in camp we separated them into species, and counted them out, and weighed them. It is pretty to see the rapidity with which the practised eye of a man of the fisherman caste will pick out the different sorts. We discarded all sorts which did not grow to over 2 lbs. in weight, and indeed busied ourselves only with such as grew to 20 lbs.; though in England any fishery law which proceeded on such lines would have to discard roach and dace and the majority of trout too. Of the fish that run to 20 lbs., *Labeo calbasu*, there were 67 in that pot, and their total weight was ten ounces, so that their individual average weight was 2·388 of a drachm; and it was at this size that they were being caught and used as food at one pie a double handful. Another equally valuable fish, *Cirrhina cirrhosa*, averaged in like manner 4·57 of a drachm and was being sacrificed in like manner.

"The owner of the cruive told me that earlier in the season his takes were very much larger, and that the sorts of fish which ran at night were different, and he particularized them. I said bring me your night take to-morrow morning, and I will buy the lot; so he did; and we separated and weighed and counted them in like manner, and made immediate notes of everything then and there.

"These examinations were instructive as well as confirmatory of the cruive owner's statements. They showed that of several sorts the fry were at that time, Christmas, well grown, so that the fry taking time was, as he said truly, drawing towards a close, and the takes earlier in the year must have been, as he said, much larger; they showed also which were the earlier spawning species, which the later. They showed also that for the purposes of the calculation which I shall hereafter base on these data, fry taken earlier in the season would have been much smaller than 4·57 and 2·388 of a drachm each, would probably have been less than a drachm each, and thus would have been much more favorable to evidencing the waste of immature fish life; for the cruive owner, it will be borne in mind, cared nothing about sorts of fish caught, he only thought of pots-full, and stated that in the earlier fry running season he got more pots-full though the fry were smaller. I only mention it here to show that the data on which I go were, as regards season, very unfavorable to my purpose.

"The data as regards locality were equally unfavorable, for the channel which I tested was one of the furthest from the breeding places of the parent fish, and was therefore calculated to have much fewer fry in it than those that tapped the breeding grounds more directly. Thus it will be seen that both in season and in locality the basis of my calculations errs strongly on the side of moderation, and that if I take this season and this stream, and assume the same proportions in other streams throughout the fry netting season I may be safely acquitted of exaggeration.

"Again I shall take only four months instead of six, because though they told me that they equally caught the fry in the two earlier months, they caught them then in the smaller channels, presumably because in the earlier two months the major channels, such as I tested, are then carrying a volume of water too strong for a cruive to be erected in. I have therefore no means of gauging the takes of the two earlier months, and rather than be led into any possible misconclusion I throw them out altogether.

"Similarly I will elect to err again on the side of moderation in the weights of fish. Though *Labeo calbasu* and *Cirrhina cirrhosa* run respectively to 20 lbs. and 10 or 15 lbs. I will take only an average of 2 lbs. each as the basis of my calculation, and with the fish taken at night also I will be chary of overestimating weights. They were *Barbus chrysopoma*, *Ophiocephalus striatus*, *O. gachua*, *Gobius giuris*, *Mastacemblus armatus* and *Cirrhina cirrhosa* again. Of these also I throw out altogether *Ophiocephalus gachua* and *Gobius giuris* as too small, though they are both great favorites with the natives, the latter especially, attaining a cubit in length and the thickness of a man's forearm and 3 lbs. in weight.

"Having then made all these deductions in favor of moderation, I take the irrigational statistics of one river in the Madras Presidency, the Cauvery with its affluents, and find that in that one river alone the immature fry destroyed and eaten when weighing only a drachm or so each represent the following fish :—

	TONS.	CWT.	LB.
Cirrhina cirrhosa weighing ...	26,162	6	8
Labeo calbasu " ...	37,932	11	78
Barbus chrysopoma " ...	1,971	2	88
Ophiocephalus striatus weighing	1,670	4	36
Mastacemblus armatus "	245	7	64
Tons	67,981	12	50

"It will be observed that in this category of fish there is not a single Mahseer, *Barbus tor*, nor a single *Barbus Carnati-*

cus, though the river abounds in them. The explanation lies in the fact that these fish breed in the upper rocky mountainous parts of the river, and my data were taken from close down to the sea. It was not in the nature of things therefore that any of them should be found in the particular cruive which I examined; but that the mighty Mahseer is also caught in other cruives higher up the river, and similarly sold for the verriest trifle at the weight of a drachm or two is an equally demonstrable fact to any one who will walk the rivers with his eyes open.

"Again it will be observed that in the above category of fish there is not a single *Wallago attu*, a Freshwater Shark that attains 6 ft. in length. The reason is that their running season was past.

"Thus both in locality and in season have my data been necessarily imperfect, giving at best but a most inadequate idea of the weight of good fish food wasted; and yet even from those inadequate data we find that, in one single river in this Presidency, there are annually destroyed by man, by means of fixed engines, at the average weight of a few drachms each, fry which if allowed a year or may be two years' grace would weigh 67,981 tons.

"The way in which all this fish life was wasted was further instructive. In this cruive they were taken quite uninjured, and nothing was easier than for the cruive owner to have selected the superior sorts and kept them alive and vigorous in a penned part of the stream, selling the inferior sorts as usual to the villagers, and getting double or treble the price for the live fry of the superior sorts from any piscicultural agency for the purpose of stocking ponds. Thus could many of the existing cruives or fixed engines be utilized for stocking ponds without being interfered with otherwise than advantageously to the cruive owners.

"I would not be misunderstood as supporting cruives altogether, for where they stand in the upper parts of rivers they ought to be prohibited; but when the water has left the river in an irrigation channel, and the fry going down the channel must eventually be dried up in a rice field and eaten by egrets, then they may as well be caught in cruives and eaten by man in preference, and in such permitted cruives, and their name is legion, the superior sorts might be saved for stocking ponds."

"But to do it a regular organization is necessary, for there are many minor practical difficulties in the way that nothing but continuous organization could overcome. For instance the carriage of fry to any distance is attended with practical difficulties which need trained agents and appliances to overcome. Only by doing it on a large scale too and systematically, could it be done really cheaply. Systematically arranged it should be possible to advertise that certain fry of superior sorts of fish, such as Mahseer, and the other larger fish mentioned above, would be delivered according to distance at a trifling price a hundred, and people wishing to stock their ponds and lakes would have it all done for them just as it is in England at a very cheap rate. For instance the Nilagiri Game Association have meritoriously set themselves to stock their Hill waters with Mahseer, and other sporting fish, and they are prepared to spend as much as Rs. 1,000 on it. Aided by a regularly organized department such as I suggest they could probably achieve equal results for a tenth of that sum, but without it they could not. Similarly many others that are not so spirited or so wealthy, and are deterred by the difficulties, and many that now know nothing about it, would find their way made easy.

"But this is only a single illustration taken from a single observation made on a fishing trip just after your note reached me."

Properly to appreciate the facilities existing in India for the capture of the fry of all sorts of freshwater fish we should stop a moment to eliminate preconceptions based on

English fish knowledge. The Salmon we know annually ascends rivers for the purpose of spawning. It has its exact parallel in India in the Hilsa. These two are sea fish seeking fresh waters for the purpose of spawning, and are classed as anadromous fish, or fish that have an upward course. None but sea fish are in England anadromous. But here in India freshwater fish as well as sea fish are highly migratory. As shewn in *The Rod in India* Mahseer are migratory within certain limits. In flood time they ascend to smaller streams which, when the floods are over, will dwindle to dimensions suitable to the strength of their diminutive fry. The fry cannot live for ever in these shallow streams; when they grow therefore they too must migrate to larger waters. And so the fry of Mahseer are exposed to capture as tiny fry in fixed basketwork traps set in every rivulet.

Other Indian fish migrate for again another reason. The marked alternations of drought and rainy seasons makes the rivers in the tropical East at one time an arid sandy bed for months and miles together, and at another time a flood that covers the country with sun-dried areas suddenly converted into extensive lakes. If Indian fish had not an intensely migratory spirit whence would all these areas of arid sandy beds and sun-baked hollows be peopled with fish life? If Indian freshwater fish were like English freshwater fish such places must remain barren of fish. But with freshwater fish of all kinds imbued with an intense spirit of migration, no sooner do the rising floods render change of place possible than they are possessed with a perfect furor to migrate in millions and millions with all their possible power. It is marvellous to see them busily migrating as if their very lives depended on it, as doubtless they do. Doubtless there would be no food for the teeming millions of fry if they were confined to the limited areas in which they were hatched. Hunger, the grand motor, is doubtless the power that drives them to migrate. It is as fry that they migrate for food, not as in England as parent fish for spawning. It is not to seek the sea as salmon par do, it is only to find fresh fields and pastures new in which they may obtain more food. Food, food, food is their cry as in countless hosts they hurry down the swelling flood.

And what is the food they get. Much doubtless that we know nothing of. But one source of food supply we do know of, one so important that I consider it the mainspring of fish life in India. I mean mosquito larvæ.

The mosquito is I hold the mainspring of fish life in India. Wherever there is moisture sheltered from wind there are mosquito ova. Wherever there is water there are hatched mosquito larvæ. Before the tiniest fry which come migrating down the overflowing streams reach any new waters that are still, those waters are thoroughly stocked in preparedness for them with an ample commissariat of mosquito larvæ, an ever present, living, rapidly reproducing food the most perfect that can possibly be desired. The first fish to migrate with the shallowest of overflows are ever the *Haplochilus panchax* (Tamil *Munda-kan-peravu*, Telugu *Āka-perigalu*) and *Haplochilus melastigma* (Tamil *Thoppu-kendai*, Telugu *Missepillalu*) diminutive *Cyprinodontidæ*, or Carp with teeth, that never grow more than an inch in length. For these the mosquito larvæ are perfect food, and they in their turn form an excellent moving commissariat for the larger fish that follow them as the waters enlarge. One of these fish has also a peculiar way of spawning. The other I have not been fortunate enough to observe. *Haplochilus panchax* extrudes one egg at a time, and that disproportionately large, as big as its own eye. This keeps hanging to the vent as the fish is moving and feeding, till it is cast and adheres. And so single eggs are laid and distributed all along the path of the migrating mother. The fry from these ova are themselves as small as the bigger mosquito larvæ. Thus is an ever preceding and ample commissariat provided, so that all the new waters are suddenly peopled with the young of fish of all sorts; and so rapid is their growth in the tropical East, teeming with insect-life, that in a single wet season many of these fish assume very edible proportions. And the mainspring of it all is the much abused mosquito.

But leaving, for the present, the mosquito, which is entitled to a chapter to itself, let us return to the fish.

After penning the above it struck me that I must have written something to the same purpose somewhere else, and looking up the preamble of a Fishery Bill drafted in October 1883 I found I had written the following which I may perhaps be allowed to quote, as it impresses from rather a different stand-point the same singularity of Indian fish, the extreme spirit of migration that comes over them with the monsoon. "As the vegetation in the tropical East is governed by the early and the latter rain, so also in varying degrees is the animal kingdom more or less affected by it, especially the fish. Confined every hot season to reduced areas decreasing with the advance of the heat, it is necessary that migration should be a leading law of their being, else how could they avail themselves for the purposes of increase of the widely extended areas suddenly covered with water by the tropical monsoon. Tropical heat and tropical rains necessarily require of Indian fish that annual migration should be a leading law of their existence.

"The Board of Revenue of 1873 wished that the Act should not be extended to "waters that are not perennial," and the Burmah Act applies only to waters that are "of a permanent nature." What such a proposition means as applied to the Madras Presidency had best be examined before it is accepted.

"It amounts to the exclusion of pisciculture from a good deal more than nine-tenths of the Presidency, it amounts to the abandonment of every river in the Presidency except two and those on the West Coast, and of some thirty thousand tanks. It amounts also to the throwing away not only of a large amount of fishery revenues formerly paid regularly, but also to a great proportion of the revenues at present collected. It is presumed that such a proposal was made only because it was conceived that in non-perennial waters we could return no equivalent advantage in the form of improved fisheries for the rents demanded. But we can render very material return, and that very easily as I shall show. And whether we can or not, still the argument stands that aqueculture is as much entitled to moderate rents in its unimproved yet naturally fertile areas as agriculture is.

"To make such a wholesale proposition is to ignore the peculiarities of the East, and to presume, without enquiry, that Indian fish similarly ignore the peculiarities of the waters of their birth. The habits of Western fish would not suit them at all, and we too must diverge from Western practice if we wish to cultivate the fish of the East. Indian fish,—I speak specially of those that have come within my own knowledge in the Madras Presidency, but I know that the description covers also a large proportion of those found in the more Northern Presidencies,—Indian fish, living as they do in tropical rivers, that are alternately a flood, a moderate stream, and a dry sand bed, accommodate themselves to the position by being much more migratory than the fish of Europe, and to allow of their being migratory their commissariat is also migratory. In England the numerous *ephemeræ* are during their larval state stationary, keeping to the water weeds, the sedges, the sand, where they were born. It is in this stationary state that they form the spring and summer food of fish more than in their ephemeral imago stage, which is very short-lived, and in which also they wander but little; the earth-worms and slugs that are washed in from the moist banks in wet weather are also stationary in their nature. In India however, though this stationary food is not wholly absent, there is a very much larger migratory element in the economy of fish food. The food of fish consists much more largely than in England of the minuter forms of fish-life, which are in far greater variety as well as in very much more minute forms than in England, so that they are of all small sizes, from less in their youth than the size of full-grown mosquito larvæ upwards. For instance one little perfectly transparent fish is at most three-fourths of an inch long, tail included, and one-eighth of an inch broad and deep when at its largest growth, with the heart, airbladder, intestine and vertibræ clearly visible through the skin when swimming. What must be its size soon after emerging from the egg which is like the finest pin-prick? So small is it that, though it has a comparatively large mouth well armed with canine teeth, it feeds on the minutest forms of water insect-life, occasionally aspiring to very juvenile mosquito larvæ, half-grown larvæ being too large for it. It requires to be watched through a magnifying glass, and as it has no name I will call it *Gobius pellucidus.* I propose to detailedly describe it elsewhere for science at better leisure, and by the aid of stronger magnifiers than I possess. Here I only mention it as markedly exemplifying the Indian principle of a migratory commissariat of living fish food accommodated to the migrations of tropical fish. Then as to variety, loaches alone number 31 species against the single *Nemachilus barbatulus* of England. Then there is the similar *Lepidocephalichtys*, and the tiny *Haplochilus*, of which two sorts *H. panchax* and *H. melastigma* are very minute and ubiquitous, and if we go to such comparatively large fish as minnows and bleak, India has some fifty to one corresponding fish, and of varied sizes, many of them much smaller than their English congeners, and in their smallness lies their usefulness, both as a food for other fish, and as being able to pass anywhere. All these are a migratory commissariat, in a perfect fidget to be moving directly the waters swell and give them opportunity. They go where the fish that man eats go, and there propagate again and again in a season. Added to these is the ubiquitous mosquito of many sorts, breeding all the year round, but breeding more at certain seasons than at others. In the least little quantity of water, in all the still margins, they hatch out in three days, and then no one can over-estimate their value as a fish food in the larval state. Fish grow and fatten on them marvellously and prefer them to anything else. They are the mainspring of fish-life in India, as well as clarifiers of water. So minute at first as almost to elude the closest scrutiny, in breadth the merest filaments and of less than the sixteenth of an inch in length, they are very soon large enough to make excellent food for a quarter of a pound fish, and then, if one in a hundred escapes, in three days more the water is repeopled with larvæ. These are doubtless the chief food of the minuter fish that are to be the food of those that feed man, and these are at hand everywhere and always, and between the two, between minute forms of fish and mosquitoes, we have every possible gradation of living, travelling commissariat from an almost imperceptible filament upwards. Then the freshwater shrimps and prawns seem, as far as I have yet noticed, to be very much more numerous in sort and variety of size than in England.

"Added to all this, we have yet another source of fish-life in mature fish (*Ophiocephaleidæ*) æstivating buried for months in the sun-baked mire of a dry tank till the floods come and release and revive them to life.

"We have also ova believed to be kept alive through drought in the same way. And the very vegetable kingdom follows the same law of adaptation to alternate flood and drought, the very rocks in the river, which have for months been so hot that one can scarce place the hand on them with comfort, are suddenly covered with verdure which forms food for the largely herbivorous fish, and food and shelter for aquatic insect-life. The frogs also (*Rana cyanophlyctis*) which have been existing on land the while, living on the insects with which India is rife, suddenly appear in multitudes on the filling of the tanks, and, unfriendly though they are to fry, make up for it by betaking themselves from the land to be food for fishes, notably for the *Ophiocephaleidæ* and *Siluridæ*. And so at a bound, a sun-dried Indian tank, thoroughly dry though it has been for months, fed by a channel from a river or stream, or from any other of a long string of tanks so fed, and even when not so fed, leaps into life, replete with all the elements of the growth and increase of fish.

"The Revenue Board of 1873 can hardly have known this when they proposed at a stroke to throw away all the non-perennial waters of Southern India. Even an ordinary English expert could scarcely be expected to know it and calculate for it; and, therefore, it is important that here in India we should not be judged in all respects by English piscicultural knowledge, nay, nor even by American, for I believe they have no frogs. But every naked Indian fisherman knows it, though he may not have thought it out in sequence; else why should they eagerly contend for the liberty of paying Rs. 2,000 a-year for the annual fishery of the river and channels of the Cauvery which are thoroughly dry for four months in the year; also why should they annually pay for the liberty to net annually sun-dried tanks? A considerable portion of the fishery revenues collected by the Engineers is derived from this source, and the practice of the natives is to postpone the fishing till just before the tank runs dry.

"By this means the minute fish and fry which have entered with the floods have time allowed them to grow up to the latest date available, and the most is made of them, some hundredweights of fish being taken out of a tank that has been perfectly dry within the twelve-month."

Seeing how the intense migratory spirit with which freshwater fish are so largely imbued in the tropical East subjects them to easy capture in fixed engines of fine basketwork, engines that span the whole channel and let none escape, it is for man to consider whether, as heretofore, they shall be captured only for wholesale destruction as fry of a drachm or two in weight, or whether this arrangement of nature should be availed of, as it so easily might be, for the distribution and culture, in convenient areas, of the more valuable sorts. To illustrate how cheaply they may be procured I may mention that without a word of bargaining fishermen spontaneously offered to supply fry of two sorts which I specified, to wit *Labeo* and *Cirrhina*, at 8 annas a 1,000.

There are many places at which they can be captured at such rates within a few yards of the places that might be stocked with them. There the matter is simple to a degree, and the marvel is that it has never been done in the Madras Presidency. When they have to be carried any distance the manner of carriage has to be considered.

In the carriage of fish the chief question is the question of crowding; but it is a simple one, and it is again a marvel that the Madras native fishermen cannot get it into their heads by practical experience, without necessarily knowing the reason of it. With the exception of the few that are direct breathers of atmospheric air, like the *Ophiocephalidæ*, fish breathe water as we breathe air, their gills extracting oxygen out of the water as our lungs do out of the air. If there are too many people in a closed room they exhaust the oxygen, and die of asphyxia, as in the Calcutta black hole. If there are too many fish in a pot of water they do the same. Water has the power of recouping itself with oxygen from the air, but only at a given rate. If the fish in the pot of water consume the oxygen in the water at a quicker rate than the water can recoup itself they must die. Reduce the number of fish in the pot to a number that cannot consume the oxygen in the water quicker than the water can recoup itself, and they will suffer no inconvenience. What is the number of fish that a pot will contain with safety to the fish is a simple matter of practical experiment dependent on the size of the pot and the size and number of the fish. If the fish are seen coming to the surface for air it is a sign they have not enough of it in the water. Their number should be decreased.

It is true that the water can be ærated mechanically, by a pair of bellows, by dipping out water and pouring it in from a height, or by constantly oscillating the pot, but it is never safe to trust to such mechanical means for any but a very short journey under reliably intelligent supervision, for if once the attendant sleeps, or otherwise neglects his charge, the whole batch perishes. On long journeys therefore be sure your fish are not overcrowded. The temptation to crowd for the sake of economy in carriage is so great that the native mind seems never able to resist it. And then they look at you with astonishment and say " they have all died," as if it was the fishes' fault.

In long journeys extending over many days fish doubtless suffer from exhaustion if they have no food as well as air; and are consequently not so strengthened as if well-fed to stand the knocking about they are called on to endure. Still it is very much better not to feed them at all than to feed them unwisely, for worms or meat or bread lying uneaten at the bottom of the vessel containing the fish, quickly putrefies and, contaminating the water, kills the fish.

The simplest and most effective way of feeding fish in transit is with mosquito larvæ. All fish take them greedily and they are small enough for the tiniest fry.

The best vehicle for carrying fish in India is a common earthen pot. Its porousness keeps the water in it cool by the evaporation always going on at the surface of the pot. Its form, narrowing towards the mouth, causes the water splashed up by any oscillation in carriage, to be thrown down again instead of splashing out, and the water thus constantly splashed up and in again is water reoxygenated. Thus the two most essential points of coolness and oxygenation of the water are obtained. The round form of the pot also presents no angles for fish to run against, and they knock themselves about much less in a round pot than in an angular vessel. They are also less likely to jump out than if the mouth were the full size of the vessel. Still they do jump out, and to prevent it the mouth should always be covered with a piece of fine meshed net. A cloth should not be used, both because it keeps out the all essential circulation of air, and also because it prevents your seeing into the pot, which you should always be able to do, because, if any of the fry die, they should be removed immediately, so that they may not contaminate the water. Be as careful as you like some of the fry are sure to die from having been injured in capture, or by handling, therefore you must be on the look out for casualties. The ones that are dieing or have recently died will be readily visible at the surface of the water; but afterwards they sink. The bottom of the pot should therefore be searched from time to time by the hand, so as to make sure that no single dead fry, however small, is allowed to remain in and contaminate the water. But the search should be made most gently both because the living fish should not be frightened and also because the dead fish will be waved away from the touch unless the movement of the hand is very slow.

The round form of the pot is against its standing up. Rings (in Tamil *perumani*) must therefore be made of some substantial material, nothing is better than rattan, and covered with straw twisted into ropes, which is soft, and so a ring is formed in which the pot easily stands. Pots will thus easily stand upright in a railway carriage. But if they require to be carried up a ghat or other place where carts cannot go they must be swung, one at each end of a springy bamboo, and the size and total weight of two pots should be not more than one man can carry.

In estimating this do not estimate for a full pot. It is a mistake to fill your pots with water. The water is sure to splash out, and you may as well arrange that for yourself by only half filling your pot at the commencement, for a half full pot encourages the wash up of the water just at the point where, from the pot beginning to narrow, the splash down again, and the consequent oxygenation, must be the inevitable result. And this constant self-working oxygenation is invaluable.

You have to bear in mind that the oxygenation from oscillation only continues as long as the fish are being moved, therefore when they come to the railway station, or to their destination, and are at rest, the time when most people would ordinarily think they are doing best, this is to the fish the most dangerous time, because the oxygenation of the water by oscillation has ceased. On no account therefore let them rest, but move them on without delay to their final resting place in the pond, lake, or stream, into which they are to be turned.

If on so turning a fish loose it has a difficulty about keeping its proper position in the water, and though struggling to regain its position is again and again turning on its side, you may frequently save such a fish, by gently holding it in its natural position in the water till in a few minutes it has recovered of its faintness and swims gaily away, whereas had you not helped it, it would have turned permanently belly upwards and died. Of course the holding must be most gently done, the fish being simply propped in position without any compression.

It has been mentioned above that in the tropical East, teeming as it is with insect and small fish life, fish grow rapidly. The following instances are indicative :—A square tank of half an acre or less in extent had been let to a contractor for fishing. He had netted it clean down to the last capturable tadpole, sparing nothing, as is their wont, and, to do it, he had, as usual, taken advantage of the close of the dry season when the tank was at its lowest. Fresh water came into that tank by a channel from the Cauvery some few days after the 15th June, certainly not earlier.

Not knowing of the netting out we went there to fish on the 29th August following. Thus not more than 75 days and more probably 70 days had intervened between the fresh stocking and our fishing. The fry-that come down these channels in the floods come, as far as my knowledge goes, not more than from 2 to 4 drachms in weight each, as shewn above (page 107). We found the tank literally full of fish, biting at times as fast as we could cast in our hooks, and we caught a goodly number wherefrom to get a fair indication of what sort of fish were in the tank, and we caught both White Carp and Labeo. We caught altogether 184, and with the exception of a very few that were smaller, and one that was larger, they all ran with remarkable closeness half a pound each. It seemed therefore that they had all entered the pond at the same size, presumedly from 2 to 4 drachms in weight, and that, as 70 days had not given much time for variations in growth, they had all attained in that time to half a pound in weight. The one that exceeded weighed a little over 1 lb. and may well have been a fry of the previous year that had escaped the net.

At another tank we had very similar experiences. It also had been netted out by a contractor. But it had had 12 or 14 months respite since the last netting, and it had been similarly stocked by the natural inflow of fry of presumedly 2 or 4 drachms each in weight within about a month of the last netting. The fish we caught were again remarkably even sized, almost all running from $1\frac{1}{4}$ to $1\frac{1}{2}$ lbs., one only to 3 lbs., and a very few being under $1\frac{1}{4}$ lb. Here again it seemed that the fish had in 12 or 13 months all grown evenly from 2 or 4 drachms to $1\frac{1}{4}$ or $1\frac{1}{2}$ lbs. in weight, the exceptional one of 3 lbs. having probably been one that had escaped netting by its then smallness.

It will be observed that the experience obtained in the second tank is strongly confirmatory of that found in the first tank, the one fish that was presumedly an escape being just the same size as all the others which had had like immunity in the second tank. In the second tank also there was the same natural accident of an escaped one, with an extra year's immunity and growth.

We noticed that the fish of $1\frac{1}{4}$ to $1\frac{1}{2}$ lbs. showed unripe roe, so that not only had they in that short time grown so remarkably rapidly, but they were already prepared to reproduce.

This last is the Rukamani Tank taken up by *The Rod in India Club*. Already full of $1\frac{1}{4}$ and $1\frac{1}{2}$ lb. Labeo and White Carp which will probably be 3 lb. fish within a year, and which will spawn in the season, the Club propose to turn in 10,000 fry before this book is in print, and to rule that all fish uuder 1 foot in length shall be put back. It will be overstocked said one in alarm. Certainly if it is not fished, but there are rods that will set that right for us. Bags like 678 lbs. to 4 rods in 3 days show both how thick these fish are able to live and thrive in a pond, and also how effectually rods can thin them. The pond that yielded that bag has had over 1,000 lbs. of fish taken out of it in a twelve-month, and yet I imagine that the fish left behind have so thriven on improved rations, in consequence of the thinning, that the total weight in the pond is probably not an ounce less than it was before it parted with its 1,000 lbs.

"The whather's *stiff* with them" is Paddy's description of a well-stocked river. The Hindu's is not so bad either. "That pond, Sir, has $\frac{3}{4}$ fish, $\frac{1}{4}$ water." A pretty stiff mixture you must admit.

Before we quit the subject of migration there is one more consideration which should not be overlooked. If Indian fry are imbued with such an overmastering spirit of migration that they come crowding down the smallest channels that lead from the streams that bred them to your ponds, equally will the same spirit impel the fry bred in your ponds to crowd out of them at the same season of the ensuing year. People stocking ponds must remember this, and carefully guard the overflow, or they will annually lose all their increase.

In answer to this objection I have heard it remarked, in connection with a piece of water that was near an estuary, that as good fish come in as go out. That of course raises the question what are the fish that will have a migratory spirit outwards, and what are the fish that are likely to come in, and what are their respective values from an angler's point of view. Generally speaking the fish that come in by the overflow will be those whose tendency is to ascend streams for breeding purposes, and they will come in as mature fish for that purpose, because the overflow runs down to them. The fish that go out will generally speaking be the fry of those very fish that came up to breed, and the parent fish themselves also, having accomplished their purpose of laying their ova, will seek to return to their ordinary habitat. In a pond overflowing into an estuary of the sea the fish that come up will naturally be such sea fish as frequent rivers to spawn in them, and among these the selection will be determined by the distance of the pond from the sea, for some sea fish such as the seer *Cybium* barely pass the river mouth, and go in and out with every tide. Others like the *Polynemus* or *Bā-mīn* and the Nair fish or cock-up (*Lates calcarifer*) go very little further; while the Mullets and the Big-eye (*Megalops*) venture greater distances from the sea, and the Hilsa (*Clupea ilisha*) runs up hundreds of miles of purely fresh water.

The fish that go out will be not only the parent fish and fry of all the sea fish that come in, but also the fry of all fresh-water fish impelled by the specially Indian spirit of migration to seek fresh fields and pastures new.

It is obvious therefore that the discharge point of your pond should be carefully guarded against the exit of fry. The simple expedient of an upright plank as shewn in *The Rod in India*, page 283, or any economical adaptation of the same principle will suffice to keep all fish in.

Allusion has been made above to "*The Rod in India Club*," an institution that I need hardly say was not so named by me, but by my too kindly friends. As it will probably interest not a few of my Madras readers to know something of its origin and objects I insert the following notice of it which appeared in *The Madras Times* of the 24th October 1887; and, in its liberal spirit of alway aiding sport, was copied *in extenso* by *The Asian.*

AN ANGLING CLUB FOR MADRAS.

In England there are Angling Clubs without number, and for all classes—both of subscribers and of fish. In North Punjab an Angling Club was some time since started; and now we learn that Madras has followed suit with a Club entitled "The Rod in India Club." The history of it is this: More than a year ago, four rods, in three days, caught 678 lbs. of fish, out of a temple tank, which had been preserved from netting. All the circumstances of the position showing clearly that the same results could be obtained in any similarly situated piece of water, the rest of the party—of whom the author of "The Rod in India" was one—urged on him the formation of a Club which would take up the preservation of waters, and form equally good fishing in a number of places conveniently dotted about the Presidency. The difficulty was, however, that only seeing is believing, and that, without seeing, few would believe what excellent sport can be had out of an Indian pond; and, even when believing it in the abstract, most of them would be disappointed in practice, as the fish are very difficult to catch till the peculiar method of angling for them is learnt. So our South Indian WALTON hesitated for fear of want of support. At the end of August last, however, privilege leave allowed of three friends meeting by the water's side, and, as they were enjoying excellent sport, they overheard that the tank was about to be netted, the owners of it only holding out in hopes of higher bids for the liberty of netting. This was too much for the anglers. Thus pushed to immediate action, they ascertained that the average income derived in the last ten years from the netting of that tank had been Rs. 42-8 a year. They offered Rs. 45 a year for 5 years certain, with liberty to add another 5 years on the same terms. It was gladly accepted. The anglers then and there formed themselves into an Angling Club, and paid down the money on the nail. The owners, seeing themselves so easily in possession of hard cash, suggested that Native contractors ordinarily gave them also a portion of fish, and that fish were very palatable to them. "All right," said the anglers, "what we want mainly is the sport, and to be quite sure of the sport not being in any way injured by poachers; your houses are all close to the tank, and if you will engage to watch the tank, and prevent all fishing by any one, European or Native, who does not hold and show you our permits, we will gladly give you an interest in watching by engaging to hand over to you half the takes." These then were the terms agreed upon, and the whole of that day's take was then and there handed over to the tank owners, to their evident satisfaction—and thus it was that "The Rod in India Club" was founded. At the time of founding, it was known that there were others who were perfectly ready to join such a Club, if only it could be started; and so they were told of it in the following circular:—

"NUNGUMBAUKAM, MADRAS, September, 1887.

"DEAR SIR,—The nucleus of an Angling Club, named 'The Rod in India Club' having been formed for the purpose of preserving waters for angling throughout the Madras Presidency, I am desired by the existing members to invite you to become a member.

"For original members the entrance donation is Rs. 25, and the annual subscription Rs. 10, which you can remit to the undersigned.

"The Club has already secured the lease of one well-stocked piece of water, and arrangements are progressing for the acquisition of more places.

(Signed) "H. S. THOMAS,
"*President and Treasurer.*"

The Club now numbers 17 members; and future members are admissible by the ordinary Club ballot. Applications for admission have to be made to the Honorary Secretary, W. WALKER, Esq., Guindy, Madras, accompanied with the entrance donation, Rs. 25, and the first year's annual subscription, Rs. 10,—in all Rs. 35. The general principle of the Club is to spend the Rs. 25 entrance donation, as far as is practicable, either in buying exclusive rights, or in stocking, or otherwise improving, fresh waters, in a neighbourhood as convenient as possible to the subscribers; the annual subscription being kept as maintenance all over the Presidency. Thus Bangalore, for instance, has waters that afford no fishing at present, but are capable of being so stocked as to yield excellent sport in a couple of years. Subscribers from Bangalore would get their entrance donations spent on the spot for them, and their annual subscription would entitle them to visit and get immediate fishing in any other of the Club's waters, till their own were good enough; and when time has effected this, then all the other subscribers chancing at any time to visit Bangalore for a holiday, or chancing to be posted there on duty, will find a new fishing ground added to the waters common to all the subscribers. We heartily wish "The Rod in India Club" all possible success; and we make bold to say, &c., &c.

The rest is too kindly complimentary.

CHAPTER VII.

THE MAINSPRING OF FISH LIFE.

"Sermons in stones and good in everything."

As You Like It.—Act II, Sc. 1.

The mosquito is, I have advanced, the mainspring of fish life in India, and as such is entitled to a chapter to itself. It so thrusts itself on our notice that it has necessarily come under the observation of many. Dr. Manson has shewn how it is the host of *Filaria sanguinis hominis*, and other writers tell us generally of its birth, growth, and habits, in connection with its being a tormentor of men and animals, and I have come across a brief newspaper notice of its killing trout. This I ought perhaps to produce in full, as it is another side of the question whether mosquitoes are beneficial to fish; and producing it I still contend that, like many another parallel, mosquitoes are the cause of infinitely much more good to fish than they are of harm. Thus there are writers not a few on the obnoxious character of the mosquito, but no one that I am aware of who has ever yet said a good word for it. I maintain however that it is an eminently useful insect, spending all the energies of its being on clarifying water, and forming the most valuable food of fish, so valuable that I consider it, as far as my knowledge goes, the mainspring of fish life in India. This I have alluded to already (page 112), and shall hope to set forth to the satisfaction of the reader. But first we should have a general outline of its course of existence. This I sat myself to work out, and had in great measure accomplished, when I found I had been anticipated by another observer. It seems due therefore to the earlier observer, Dr. Gilchrist, that I should give you the life history of the mosquito in his words, rather than in my own, as penned by him and printed in the *Journal of Literature and Science* published by the Madras Literary Society in July 1837, premising that, for the sake of my page, I have had slightly, but very slightly, to reduce the size of his drawings.

ON THE METAMORPHOSES OF THE MUSQUITO.

By W. Gilchrist, Esq., of the Madras Medical Establishment.

The following are a few observations I lately made on the successive forms the musquito assumes, before becoming the troublesome insect known under that name. Not having, at present, an opportunity of learning whether they add any thing new to the natural history of the insect, I trust, if they do not, this communication may be put aside.

The musquito has three stages of existence, in two of which it is a water insect, in the third the well-known winged one—6th May, 6 A.M. I observed several musquitoes on the surface of some stagnant water, each in close proximity to a yellowish substance, which, when viewed through a microscope, proved to be a collection of eggs that the musquitoes were depositing; each collection, though consisting of not fewer than one hundred eggs, did not exceed three-twentieths of an inch in length, and about one-twentieth of an inch in breadth. These eggs were arranged in lines, standing on end, and were each about one fortieth of an inch long: the lower end being larger than the upper, so that the upper surface of the collection was somewhat concave.

A few of these collections of ova were carefully introduced, with some of the water on which they floated, into a tumbler, and placed under a glass shade. Excepting a change of colour, from a yellow to a dark brownish grey, which occurred within six hours after being put into the tumbler, no visible alteration took place, till two days and a half, when the water was found to swarm with animalculæ. The shells of the ova were still adherent, as when first observed. On examining one minutely, the larger, or under, end was found to have opened, like a lid, to allow the insect to escape into the water. A lady's thimble, furnished with a lid, would resemble exactly the appearance of what is being described. The design of having the lids placed at the bottom, is, evidently, to allow the newly-hatched animalculæ immediate exit from the shell into the water; and the concavity of the whole collection, above alluded to, effectually tends to retain the large ends undermost. Had the ova been arranged promiscuously, as to the large and small ends being upwards and downwards, it is evident that the newly-hatched insect, under the former arrangement, would have some difficulty in reaching the water, a difficulty that, most probably, would amount to an impossibility; one which, at all events, is effectually prevented by the concave form of the collection.

A sketch of the newly-hatched insect, about 2,500 times the natural size, is given in Figure 1. In the chest or thorax (*a*), the heart is seen (obscurely however, the body being only semi-transparent), furnished with four projections; from this organ two blood-vessels proceed down the centre of the body, to the end of the elongation (*b*), the extreme termination of which is to be seen just above the surface of the water, where the insect lives, for the most part; the body being suspended, as it were, from this, head lowermost.

Between the heart, in the thorax, and the extremity of this singular elongation, an active sanguiferous circulation is to be observed; in all probability, therefore, it is the seat of the lungs or gills, and it would appear that a comparatively large supply of air, is essential to the existence of the insect, as it lives, as much as possible, in this pendulous position at the surface, with the extremity of the elongation rising just above.

Its motion, which is quick, is effected by a rapid bending of its whole body, so that head and tail (the latter represented at *c*), and consisting of a bundle of delicate filaments, approximate, alternately, on either side of the body; it always goes tail foremost, so that the head is dragged along behind. When in search of food, it throws out, in advance of its mouth, a couple of delicate brushes, the individual filaments of which, though seen magnified to the extent above stated, were still of microscopic size. The oval-shaped figures in the head (*d*, Fig. 1) represents these brushes when not in use (though obscurely, as the semi-transparent body intervenes). Each of these is put in rapid circular motion, whereby a double kind of whirlpool is occasioned; whatever food comes within the sphere of these vortices, is speedily devoured. The food appears to be, principally, decomposing vegetable matter, some of which I put into the tumbler, as the vessel in which the ova were discovered contained it; on this they fed voraciously. They did not, however, entirely confine themselves to a vegetable diet. I was much amused with one, when in a drop of water under the microscope; in these confined limits its appetite did not forsake it, and the only article of food it found was the head of one of its own species. So soon as this came within the vortex, it was ravenously seized, but, being, apparently, too large a *morceau*, it was let go, after sundry futile attempts at swallowing. It frequently came within the whirlpool

Plate XVII

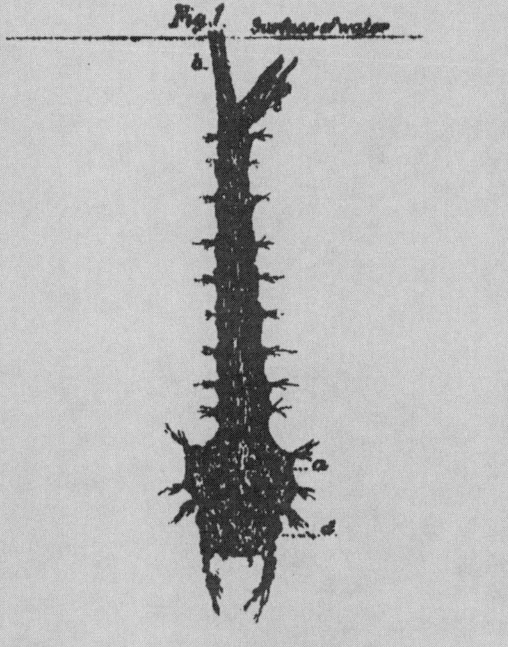

MOSQUITO LARVÆ

again, and was as often seized, but with no better success. They, however, eat the shells they had recently quitted. Some that were kept in clean water, without food, died on the third day. In this stage of their existence, the insects were lively and grew apace.

At the termination of 21 days, during which the water was thrice changed, they had attained three or four-twentieths of an inch in length. On attaining this size, or age, they underwent a second metamorphosis. The shape they assumed is represented in Figure 2, magnified, like the former 2,500 times. Most likely they cast their former envelope, for the hairs, so conspicuous on the former insect, were not to be seen on the present. The shape, it will be remarked, has materially altered, but the most remarkable change is that which occurs with respect to the seat of the lungs or gills. These organs are now situate in the thorax, their former seat (the elongation *b*, fig. 1) has disappeared, and the channel of communication, now, between them and the air, are two small tubes (*b*, fig. 2) on the top of the chest. In this stage of their existence, the insects are much less active than during the former one. A still greater contrast, however, is that, now, they do not require food, and have no mouth; in this respect resembling the chrysalis stage of the butterfly tribe. But the demand for air appears increased; they rarely leave the surface of the water, and, when they do descend, they take down a supply of air, small globules of which are distinctly to be observed, at the end of the tube (*b*, fig. 2). Their descent is accomplished by striking the water with their body, but, being specifically lighter than that fluid, they rise without any effort to the surface, though, in case of *despatch*, can impel themselves upwards by the same means as they descended. However, as has been remarked, they seldom leave the surface, and, having done so, speedily return to it.

The insects remain about 48 hours in this stage; towards the termination of which the legs and proboscis of the winged musquito can be distinctly seen through the thin membrane that surrounds it. This, in due course, bursts, when the winged musquito draws itself out, stands on the surface of the water a few minutes, to dry and expand its wings, on which it presently proceeds to a dry situation. I observed several undergoing this change.

If the musquito, when in either of the first two stages, be taken out of the water, it speedily dies, and it is as speedily deprived of life, if immersed in that fluid immediately after becoming the winged insect.

We learn from the above, that the musquito is a most prolific insect and that, as stagnant water such as that of tanks, &c., is necessary to its propagation, all such ought to be kept as distant as possible from our dwellings; whereby we are more likely to enjoy an immunity from their annoyance, than by practising the mode so facetiously described, or rather suggested, by Captain Basil Hall in his voyages.

There are many sorts of mosquitoes, how many is probably not known. Dr. Gilchrist does not tell us which of the mosquitoes it is of which he writes, and all my earlier observations were unfortunately made with the same want of definition of species, I have therefore to start again to be specific. But in the meantime Dr. Gilchrist's observations, like my own, are sufficient general guide to illustrate our present argument.

As promised above once more will I quote from others before proceeding to my own remarks.

MOSQUITOES KILLING TROUT.

A recent *Bulletin* of the United States Fish Commission contains the following interesting account of the destruction of young trout by mosquitoes:—"In the middle or latter part of June, 1882, I was prospecting on the head-waters of the Tumichie Creek, in the Gunnison Valley, Colorado. About nine o'clock in the morning I sat down in the shade of some willows that skirted a clear but shallow place in the creek. In a quiet part of the water, where their movements were readily discernible, were some fresh-hatched brook or mountain trout, and circling about over the water was a small swarm of mosquitoes. The trout were very young, still having the pellucid sack puffing out from the region of the gills, with the rest of the body almost transparent when they would swim into a portion of the water that was lighted up by direct sunshine. Every few minutes these baby trout—for what purpose I do not know, unless to get the benefit of more air—would come to the surface of the water, so that the top of the head was level with the surface of the water. When this was the case a mosquito would light down and immediately transfix the trout by inserting its proboscis, or bill, into the brain of the fish, which seemed incapable of escaping. The mosquito would hold its victim steady until it had extracted all the life juices, and when this was accomplished, and it would fly away, the dead trout would turn over on its back and float down the stream. I was so interested in this before unheard-of destruction of fish that I watched the depredations of these mosquitoes for more than half an hour, and in that time over 20 trout were sucked dry and their lifeless bodies sent floating away with the current. It was the only occasion when I was ever witness to the fact, and I have been unable by inquiry to ascertain if others have observed a similar destruction of fish. I am sure the fish were trout, as the locality was quite near the snow line, and the water was very cold, and no other fish were in the stream at that altitude. From this observation I am satisfied that great numbers of trout, and perhaps infant fish of other varieties in clear waters, must come to their death in this way; and if the fact has not been heretofore recorded, it is important to those interested in fish culture."

These notices, showing that mosquitoes are bred wherever there is water, and that they kill trout fry, are both in the direction of their obnoxious character. I desire to pursue the subject from another point of view, that of their usefulness as a food for fish. What is the use of a mosquito is the puzzle that has often confronted the thinker. Let us see.

When first hatched from the egg the larvæ of the mosquito are, like hairs, so short and so fine that they are scarcely visible without a glass; indeed they would not be visible but for their constant motion. At that age they are small enough for the minutest fry of the minutest sort of fish, to wit the tiny *Haplochili*, to devour with ease. As they grow they attain in this their earlier stage to as much as a quarter of an inch in length of body, exclusive of filaments. This is the size of the small mosquito that has clearly marked white bars on its black legs. There are other mosquitoes of which the larval forms are decidedly larger. But these small ones even are taken with avidity by every fish that I ever saw near them, from fry of half an inch in length to 5 lb. fish. Everything that swims seems to feed on them and with avidity. Given to gold fish, Gourāmī, Carnatic Carp, Mahseer, and a variety of other fish, they are hunted about and picked off in the most greedy manner. Fish will forsake worms for them by preference. Again and again have I tested it in a variety of ways that may interest and serve to convince my readers.

I had a large aquarium which I was preparing for fish, but which I had been too busy to attend to for some days, when I noticed that it was swarming with mosquito larvæ, and it was obvious that we should have the house full of hatched out mosquitoes in a few hours. A few small *Haplochili* were easily introduced, and in an hour's time the aquarium was thoroughly cleared of mosquito larvæ.

When lately sending Mahseer fry by request to Ceylon, though by the way it has since been discovered that they have them indigenous, it was on mosquito larvæ that I relied entirely for their food. When first caught and kept in pots till their numbers were made up it was on mosquito larvæ that they were fed. When they came off their rail journey of 327 miles from Mettapolliam to Madras, which they did at an hour when my engagements would not admit of my meeting them myself, I simply told my native servant "see they have a good dinner when they come in." He knew from old experience that for fish a good dinner must mean mosquito larvæ, and could not possibly mean anything else, and answered in that sense at once: and when the young Mahseer arrived there were tens of thousands of mosquito larvæ awaiting them. The next morning I looked them all over myself, and gave them their *chota hazari* (early meal) of the same, and, that they might not faint by the way, when putting them on board the steamer from Madras to Ceylon, I sent an extra potful of refreshments of the same sort, and the man in charge was instructed, on arrival at Colombo, to obtain a fresh supply in the bazaar and give the fry a substantial meal thereof before calling on them to undertake the fatigues of the railway journey from Colombo to Newara Ellaya. This he did, and the result was that out of 21 Mahseer fry shipped from Madras to Newara Ellaya 19 reached their mountain stream well and vigorous, the two that failed failing by reason of extra vigour, jumping out of their pots where the covering net had got displaced.

Sending Mahseer and Carnatic Carp fry by a long rail and road journey from Mettapolliam to the Pulney Hills it was again mosquito larvæ that were relied on, with the result that 60 Carnatic Carp and 19 Mahseer reached their destination, without a casualty, well and vigorous. One Carnatic Carp only was weakly, but it recovered: the others were all not only alive but vigorous. Does my reader feel better ordinarily after a good dinner? So did they. A railway journey of 242 miles at 20 miles an hour, and a road journey of 47 miles carried by men at a foot's pace is not to be undertaken without refreshments.

The great advantage of the mosquito larvæ is that they may be trusted as a food to any uninstructed person, because there is no fear of over-doing them. If more than the fish can possibly eat are put in no harm is done. Their element is water and they continue to live in it. Indeed they do good, for their office is to clarify water, and living in the water, they continue to do their office till the satiated fish are again hungry, and take them as food. From their being always present in the water the fish feed on them leisurely from time to time at will, which is much more natural than enforced periods of fasting and gorging, dependent on the whim or erring judgment of the human feeder in supplying them with what he considers the right modicum of food at the right distances of time. By such natural feeding with mosquito larvæ fish are not only kept alive, but in full natural vigour.

In hand-feeding the fish are not evenly fed, for the young and weakly dare not feed till the stronger and larger are satisfied, and then perhaps the attendant holds his hand in fear of overdoing it, lest a portion of food should be left unconsumed to poison the water for the whole batch. No such results need be feared with mosquito larvæ. Not only do the surplus larvæ continue to live till the weakly also have leisurely had their fill, but they meanwhile diligently ply their office of clarifying the water; and the fish fœces are food enough for them.

That clarifying the water is their office is clearly traceable from their surroundings. Where is it that they are found? In any still water. But where in the greatest numbers? Where the water is foulest. Where some fetid drain discharges, there are they in countless numbers. There it is that my servants seek them when sent for a supply. The fouler the water the more the larvæ rejoice in it. You may find them luxuriating in water that is so black with decaying matter that you would think it was impossible for anything to live in it. Put them in pure water and Dr. Gilchrist tells us they starve. I confess I have not noticed this myself. Perhaps he used distilled water. I did not. I have seen them in a tub that had still the smell of paint on it. The fish that were in it had to be promptly removed to save their lives as they were turning over. Not so the mosquito larvæ. They were none the worse for the paint smell. I have even dropped phenyle into the water without seemingly affecting them. They may be easily observed in a thin blown glass tumbler of water. When at rest they affect the surface; when disturbed they seek shelter at the bottom, quickly returning to the surface if left alone. Drop a piece of meat in and they will follow it to the bottom, and you will see them diligently at work on it. Let it putrefy and float, they follow it still at the surface. Transfer them with water to the microscope and you will see their two nippers for holding food, while two round bristle-edged blades are protruded to cut it. These circular blades are protruded and drawn in at pleasure, and even when drawn in may be seen through the semi-transparent head to be working away busily. Extreme voracity seems to be the characteristic of the earlier larval form, and decaying matter its food. I have not seen that the larvæ attack other insect-life. This is the earlier stage that I speak of. In the second stage, which answers in a measure to the chrysalis stage they have no mouth, and the two long tubes proceeding from the back rather than the chest and ending each in a funnel-shaped cup are ever taking in atmospheric air direct at the surface: and if the larvæ descend they do so always head upwards, and two silvery bubbles, one in each cup-shaped nostril, are discernible. In this stage fish take them just as freely as in the earlier stage, and in bulk, though shorter and thicker, they are about the same then, as they were just before their transformation from the earlier stage.

Though this second stage answers to the chrysalis stage, it is not a dormant stage by any means, only a stage in which the animal takes no food, for the necessities of its position in a moving fluid like water demand that the insect shall be able to adjust its position by motion, and so it jerks itself downwards by its tail when it chooses, and when motionless returns spontaneously to the surface by its specific gravity being less than that of water. It has no power of swimming laterally without its tail as the earlier larval form can in search of food. It has parted with the numerous projecting filaments the earlier larvæ have.

The larvæ in the second stage have but two flukes set on transversely as in the whale, and presumably for the same purpose of enabling it to reach the air rapidly. The larvæ in the earlier stage have four flanges to the tail, two long and two short, which work independently and seemingly facilitate giving direction in swimming.

The larvæ in the second stage can move their funnel-shaped nostrils as deer do their ears, and they have a tuft of short filaments on their back which would seem to answer the purpose of a dorsal fin in keeping the back and hence the nostrils uppermost.

The larvæ shed their cases both from the earlier into the second stage and from the second into the fly stage, and these shed cases sink to the bottom and form food for the younger larvæ. So do the fœces of fish and water snails which always sink to the bottom, while those of terrestrial animals have a tendency to float. Whether at the surface or at the bottom the mosquito larvæ attack it, and exert themselves to the utmost in clearing it off.

Under the microscope many insects exhibit proportions and offensive weapons which are so formidable in their strength as to be almost repellent. Not so the black and white-barred mosquito of Southern India; under the microscope it is an exquisitely beautiful insect. Hatch one out in a tumbler under your own eye so that you may have it all uninjured, and as it stands on its chrysalis case, only just emerged therefrom, paralyse it with a good whiff of tobacco smoke, keeping the smoke in by closing the mouth of the tumbler with paper. Then removing the mosquito most delicately, still alive but paralysed, place it under the microscope, and you will see that from head to foot it is beautifully feathered all over. The black parts are a complete coat of black feathers, the white bars are wholly composed of closely ranged white feathers. The beautiful markings on the head are all made of feathers. The whole body is simply coated all over with feathers, and each separate feather is a study in itself as some of them come off in removing the mosquito, and lie separate on the glass, each with its quill attachment at its base. The very wings too are feathered, but differently. Here the feathers are grey to accord with the transparent gauze wings; and they are longer and thinner than those on the body; by far the longest and the finest are those that are disposed in a close set fringe all round the edge of each wing, the numerous ribs of the wings are also furnished each with beautifully regular rows of long thin feathers. So fine are they, and so easily disturbed by a breath of air, that till very closely examined they have the appearance of *filaria* sometimes in life-like motion.

Different mosquitoes are feathered differently. The one

above described is as I have said the small black and white-barred one of Southern India. It has in coloring a close general similarity to the West Indian mosquito *Culex Mosquito*, but it differs in several details, and from its zebra-like black and white marking may perhaps be distinguished as *zebraicus*, while from its *palpi* being shorter than the proboscis it would seem to be not *Culex* but *Œdes zebraicus.* A small brown mosquito of about the same size has several characteristics similar to those of the common English gnat, *Culex pipiens*, but closer examination than I have been able to give it will doubtless show it to be again a distinct species. At present I wish only, in the above connection, to refer to the feathering. This brown mosquito is marked also with varied colourings which turn out on inspection to be composed of feathers, but it is not nearly so closely feathered as *Œdes zebraicus.* The top of its head has no feathers on it, but is covered instead with coarse brown hairs. The proboscis of this brown mosquito is like that of the gnat *Culex pipiens* while the proboscis of our black and white mosquito *Œdes zebraicus* is like that of the West Indian mosquito, *Culex Mosquito.* *Œdes zebraicus* has protruding from its back behind the wings one pear-shaped sac, which is to be found in both males and females. But the brown gnat-like mosquito has not got it. I do not profess to have studied this sac but an American writer has made a most minute and interesting study of a somewhat similar pair of "*pyriform capsules*" (*i.e.* pear-shaped little chests) in *Culex Mosquito*, which he terms confidently "the auditory capsule." I have confined myself, as my time and opportunities barely admit, to the practically useful side of the question, the *use* of the mosquito, being only tempted to diverge from time to time as marvels of beautiful structure thrust themselves across my path, and I only mention them here to instance what a wide and beautiful study the mosquito might be in India to any one who had sufficient time and opportunity to follow it up thoroughly.

I can conceive no more beautiful set of slides for the microscopist than a complete set of the several organs of the several species of mosquitoes in India. But any such study would be incomplete indeed if it confined itself to the forms and faculties of the insect in its short-lived winged stage, and neglected its much longer and useful existence in the water. The very interesting American writer above referred to has with admirable exactness entered in painstaking detail into all the minutiæ of the winged insect, and yet leaves his reader sadly disappointed that such an exact observer,* while giving so much attention to one-tenth of the mosquito's existence, the one-tenth which, as far as we know, is devoted to the annoyance of man and beast, and to no useful purpose but that of propagation, while he entirely neglects the other nine-tenths of its life which are diligently employed in clarifying water, and in being, as I contend, the mainspring of fish life in India.

It is presumable that the mosquito in its aquatic forms is equally useful to fish life in other lands, and it is not a little with a view to provoke to this enquiry the advanced pisciculturists of the United States that these remarks are put forward.

It is recorded of the common gnat that it lays 200 or 300 eggs a year. My impression is that the Indian mosquito lays about the same number every month, that is to say that a mosquito during its life of three days lays 200 or 300 eggs, which within a month have hatched and grown from larvæ to mosquitoes which are again laying 200 or 300 eggs, to be again matured within the month. But if we limit our layings to 100 eggs, the number which Dr. Gilchrist counted in a single raft of eggs, and suppose immunity from destruction we arrive at the following astounding figures, and the compari-

* Dr. Christopher Johnston, Quarterly Journal of Microscopical Science.

sons which follow may be allowed me for illustrating what a power in the matter of fish life the tiny little mosquito is.

One female mosquito laying at the commencement of the year 100 eggs, would, at the end of the month, be found the parent of 100 mosquitoes of which 50 would be females. In the second month 50 females laying each 100 eggs would yield 5,000 larvæ. In the third month 2,500 females × 100 eggs = 250,000 larvæ. In the fourth 12,500,000 larvæ and so on till at the end of the twelve-month there would be 488,281,250,000,000,000,000 larvæ. Astonishing figures doubtless but well kept in countenance by the fertility of the blue bottle fly and the herring, about which computations have been made that the former, if not preyed upon, would in a year cover the earth's surface with its progeny, I think it was a foot thick, and that the latter would girdle the earth's circumference in 10 years I think it was with a wall I am afraid to say how high and how thick. I think it was 100 feet. But to repeat such things from memory is of course utterly unreliable and I regret I cannot find my notes of them and my authorities. However if the curious reader likes to work out the above figures of the mosquito larvæ so as to give his mind a definite impression he will find that the total length of 488,281,250,000,000,000,000 larvæ, each a quarter of an inch long, will be 77,377,195,092 times round the earth's greatest circumference taken at 24,899 miles, and more than 21 million times the distance from the earth to the sun taking 91,430,000 as the sun's distance.

But such figures are extravagant. All I desire to do is to get the mind of the reader to accept generally that the insignificant mosquito is a mighty power in producing food for fish.

I do not say positively that it is within my knowledge that any particular Indian mosquito breeds at the rate above indicated. I only say that mosquitoes of some sort are present with us and reproducing their species all the year round, that their rate of production as far as it is known is not under 100 eggs a laying, and that I cannot remember ever having noticed the absence of my little friend *Œdes zebraicus* for instance. Still I know there are some seasons when certain mosquitoes, not seen at others, make their appearance; and it is not improbable also that different species may affect different localities. For instance while I am writing I have around me in my country residence *Œdes zebraicus* and the little brown mosquito above described, and which answers generally to Manson's brief description of the one that he found to be host to *Filaria sanguinis hominis;* while at the same time a much larger mosquito is noticeable among the open drains of the native bazaar of the town of Madras and, while correcting the proofs, another one with brown spots upon its wings has put in an appearance. In the moist climate of Burmah they are exceptionally large and venomous so that we are told on grave authority that at certain places the very horses have to be protected by mosquito nets. My belief is that the different sorts of mosquitoes are far more numerous than is generally imagined, and that the probabilities are in favor of my figures being borne out by one or more of the several species of mosquito with which the tropical East abounds, and that the subject is worth working out by those who have the appliances and the leisure. I commend it to our Madras Professor of Biology, and I trust the advanced pisciculturists of the United States will consider it worthy of their attention.

Given a rate of reproduction any way approximating the figures which I have put forward, and given a scientifically thought out and properly constructed mosquito hatching house, in which the mosquito and the larvæ would be given immunity from the ordinary vicissitudes of nature, conceive what an enormous unmeasurable supply of the most excellent fish food could be kept always ready at hand. The supply could be made illimitable, it could probably be produced infinitely more cheaply than any other food, and I think I may say without fear of contradiction that it would be food far better suited to young fish than any that is now known, and I am sure none could be more conveniently portable for feeding fish on a journey.

I have found in my experiments that while any small tumbler will suffice for the rearing of the larvæ, the same covered with a card board will not do for the winged insects because there is in it no food for them. But if the mouth of the tumbler is covered with muslin, and a piece of raw meat placed on the muslin, the mosquitoes may be seen settled on it with the proboscis inserted through the meshes of the muslin. But circumstances prevented this experiment being carried to a conclusion, and it is probable that while some mosquitoes take kindly to raw mutton, others may prefer that aquatic and other plants should be living and growing within their reach.

Before we leave them to those who have better leisure and better appliances for thorough study than one in my official position can ever hope for, I will mention one or two more little details that dropped across my path.

As Manson tells us, tobacco smoke may be conveniently used for temporally paralysing and facilitating the uninjured capture of the otherwise too active mosquito. But it can easily be overdone in a closed vessel like a covered tumbler, and then death is the speedy result. The fumes have the same effect, though in a somewhat less degree, on the air breathing larvæ.

The male mosquito is easily distinguishable from the female, not only by its following the ordinary law of insects in being very much smaller than the female, a matter noticeable with the naked eye, but also in the appearance of the head. The female of *Œdes zebraicus* has two long fine antennæ like two single hairs, the male has two short broad plumes. This may be seen by the naked eye of some, under an ordinary hand glass by any one. Placed under the microscope it will be seen that the long thin autennæ of the female are covered with hairs all the way up, and that the short plumes of the male consist of a central rib with long lateral ribs or feathers very like an ostrich plume. This difference in the sexes I find recorded as common to all the family *Culicides* "antennæ filiform, covered with hairs—in the male sex resembling little plumes." The male of our zebra like mosquito has on each side of the proboscis two feelers (*palpi*) half the length of the proboscis. I do not trace them in the female. Thus the male with his plumes and two feelers uniting with the proboscis, may be readily distinguished through a hand glass from the female with her fine antennæ. I have watched through a glass as they sat busy on my hand, for I have been interested to discover if it is true that it is only the female that attacks us, the male being too shy. As yet it is only the female that I have been able to observe in the act of inserting its proboscis, still I have seen many males all too much at home in my house, and I fancy they are not entitled to a verdict of acquittal till the case has been remanded for further enquiry.

Maribus, fere intra caudam cavam, potest videri duplex membrum ad prehendendum aptum, sed inversum. His animalculis volantibus coitus fit, ventre ventri opposito.

When the mosquito is born it lays its eggs sometimes on a floating leaf of water lily, sometimes on the water itself where the eggs float; and in the rich profusion of nature seemingly almost anywhere. They have been observed laid in the folds of clothes hung on a clothes horse, and the larvae have by a competent observer been seen to be hatched there, and from this it has been conjectured that there may be mosquitoes which are propagated without water. There may be doubtless, but in this case they were not followed up to see if they were merely hatched out by damp, and died for want of water or continued to live without it. Till it is conclusively shewn to the contrary the presumption is that the larvæ of all mosquitoes are aquatic.

I have said above that wherever there is moisture there are mosquito larvæ. But more than this there are eggs in a multitude of places where the chances of nature may possibly bring water to them. In the form of ova they are doubtless able to withstand drought waiting till the water shall reach them and hatch them out. This I am wishing to put to tests, but have not yet had the leisure. This at least we k ow that when the water does reach them they are quickly hatched out into larvæ which people the waters in every little hollow.

Every one knows the mosquito, and every one in India is conversant with the little wriggling forms to be seen in any water, in the very saucers placed at the foot of a meatsafe to keep out the ants. But many do not know that these wriggling forms are the larvæ of mosquito. They will now recognize them by the plate.

In this larval form I tried certain experiments on them, wishing to find a way by which I could suspend their animation, so that when sending a batch of fish on a long sea or rail journey I could send with them a batch of mosquito larvæ to be indented on from time to time for their food. If I sent the larvæ alive in water they answered excellently for the ordinary term of their existence, but at the end of that they hatched out and became mosquitoes and left me. Also my friends might not thank me for sending them mosquitoes in a winged state. So I wanted to suspend the animation of the larvæ so as to retard their hatching out.

I tried the usual thing, hybernation by means of cold by the use of ice. But they always died.

I was not surprised, and then tried œstivation as more suited to a tropical clime. Draining the water in which the larvæ were through flannel, I left the flannel to dry: and so I dried them for varying periods from 24 hours to six days. In the heat of the hot season they were thoroughly desic-

19

cated in a very short time, and to all appearance dead. But on being put into water they recovered within a minute. I found that those in the second or chrysalis stage not infrequently hatched out under desiccation, and that of the others those which stood the treatment best were the smallest. But the percentage that survived 6 days of absolute desiccation was small.

From these experiments I concluded that ova, even if unseasonably hatched out by an occasional shower, would exist in the smallest drop of remaining water, and even if that were dried up, could still survive the accident for some days of drought in their earlier stage till there came a second shower or even a heavy dew and revived them, and so they held on till the country was covered with water and their season commenced.

But it is doubtless in the form of ova that they can best stand the vicissitudes of drought, waiting till moisture shall animate them to enter on their useful life as food for fishes. As ova they do not need to eat and breathe as they do as larvæ, and adhering where they are deposited wait till moisture liberates them. How long this period of waiting can be prolonged at will by man is a point which I have wanted to test; but I have not had the leisure, and it is not easy to collect the ova. I must leave the continuance of the experiment to those with more leisure than myself, having I hope sufficiently indicated that their lies in it enough of beauty to interest the abstract student and microscopist, and that on the pisciculturist the mosquito has a special claim to his best attention as a mighty power in the feeding of fish.

CHAPTER VIII.

NAMES, DESCRIPTION AND HABITAT OF FISH.

THE following highly epitomized extracts from Dr. Day's "Fishes of India" may be useful in aiding recognition of the fish treated of in this volume, in showing the areas over which they are respectively spread, the sizes they attain, and the vernacular names which Dr. Day attaches to them. I have given not only those known to have been actually taken by the methods described in the previous pages, but also those likely to be so taken, distinguishing the latter by remarks. In order to complete the list of fish to be taken with a hook in Indian fresh waters and estuaries I have added also those treated of in *The Rod in India*, distinguishing them also by brief remarks. All fish that do not attain a pound in weight or a foot in length have been omitted, unless they have merited exceptional notice by reason of their being fly takers; and even there I have had to hold my hand somewhere, omitting the Indian minnow though he is an excellent little fly taker; and I have seen lunatics enthusiastic over them. Any brief additions that I may make to the epitomes of Dr. Day's text will be recognizable at once by the difference in type.

Vernacular nomenclature presents very great difficulties, not only because the same fish has different names in so many different Indian languages, but also because the same language gives it different names in different localities, as well as at different ages, just as the salmon has a multitude of synonyms in the English language. Moreover when we have succeeded in linking the right vernacular to the right scientific name, so very few transliterate it systematically, so that the true pronunciation is lost in haphazard spelling. Consequently vernacular naming is sadly unreliable, though if it could be correctly ascertained it would be a much easier guide to the great majority of beginners than the scientific descriptions which alone are accurate. In the names that follow I shall add my mite in the direction of correct vernacular nomenclature, in the hope that it may provoke others to further it. And to aid their transliterating on a known system I give briefly the essence of that approved by the Madras Government.

Following the system originally recommended by Sir William Jones and since adopted with partial variations by the Asiatic Society, the Madras Literary Society, and by Professor Wilson in his Glossary of Indian official terms, the Madras Government in 1859 directed its officers to adopt the following vowel scale in transliterating from the vernaculars to Roman letters:—

Short	ă or a	as	the	a in about and delta.
Long	ā	„	„	long a in father.
	ĭ or i	„	„	i in pin.
	ī	„	„	long i is in pique.
	ŭ or u	„	„	oo in good.
	ū	„	„	long oo in moon.
	ĕ or e	„	„	e in mendicant (nearly the French é).
	ē	„	„	ey in grey (nearly the French ê).
	ai	„	„	ai in aisle or ei in height.
	ŏ or o	„	„	o in police.
	ō	„	„	long o in story or prose.
	au	„	„	ou in foul or ow in down.

To assist the uninitiated in following the fish formulæ I append the following:—

B. iii = Branchiostegals iii.
D. = Dorsal fin.
P. = Pectoral „
V. = Ventral „
A. = Anal „
C. = Caudal „
L. l. = Lateral line.
L. tr. = „ transverse.

Lates calcarifer.

Dangara, Sind.; *Nuddee-meen* or *Nair-meen*, Mal.; *Painnee-meen* or *Koduwa*, Tam.; *Pandu-kopah* or *Pandu-menu*, Tel.; *Durruah* and *Bekkut*, Ooriah; *Begti*, Beng.; *Nga-tha-dyk*, Arrac.; *Koral*, or if large *Baor*, Chittagong; *Todah*, Andam.; *Cock-up* of Europeans.

B. vii, D. $7-8/\frac{1}{11-12}$, P. 17, V. 1/5, A. $\frac{3}{8-9}$, C. 17, L. l. 52—60, L. tr. 6—7/13, Cæc. pyl. 3.

HABITAT.—Seas, backwaters, and mouths of tidal rivers in the East, up which last it often ascends long distances to prey upon its weaker neighbours. It is excellent eating when from the vicinity of large rivers. It salts well, and from it some of the best "Tamarind-fish" is prepared.

To be taken spinning with a dead fish or spoon in the estuaries, as described in *The Rod in India*, where it is also figured. The Canarese name is *Kulanji* when small, *Madāvu* when large. The Malayalim name *Koolon*. It runs to over 30 lbs. in weight.

Lutianus roseus.

B. vii, D. $\frac{10}{14}$, P. 16, V. 1/5, A. $\frac{3}{8}$, C. 17, L. l. 48, L. r. $\frac{57}{50}$, L. tr. 7/18.

HABITAT.—Seas of India to the Malay Archipelago.

The Canarese name is *Kemb-ēri*. Runs to 5 lbs. and perhaps more. To be taken spinning in estuaries. *Rod in India*, page 213, where it is also figured.

Polynemus Indicus.

Tahlun-kala, Tam.; *Yeta*, Mal.; *Dara*, Bombay; *Bhāt*, Mahr.; *Lukwah*, Arrac.; *Katha* or *Ka-ku-yan*, Burm.; *Kwey-yeng*, Tavoy.

B. vii, D. $8/\frac{1}{13-14}$, P. 15 + v, V. 1/5, A. $\frac{2-3}{11-12}$, C. 17, L. l. 70—75, L. tr. 7/13, Vert. 5/19, Cæc. pyl. many.

HABITAT.—Seas of India to the Malay Archipelago and Australia. It attains 4 feet in length, but is rarely above 20 lbs. weight. A large fish yields about two ounces of rough isinglass. The largest specimens appear to be captured in the embouchures of large rivers: they take a bait freely.

Polynemus tetradactylus.

Polun-kala, Tam.; *To-bro-dah*, Andam.

B. vii, D. $8/\frac{1}{13-15}$, P. 17 + iv, V. 1/5, A. $\frac{2-3}{15-17}$, C. 17, L. l. 75 — 85, L. tr. 8/14, Cæc. pyl. many.

HABITAT.—Seas of India to the Malay Archipelago and China, attaining 6 feet and upwards in length: it is excellent eating. This species appears to ascend higher up the rivers than any of the others, and the young are numerous in the Hooghly at Calcutta. Ham. Buchanan observes: "I have been assured by a credible native that he saw one which was a load for six men, and which certainly therefore exceeded in weight 320 lbs. Avoirdupois. (Fish Ganges, p. 225.)

This is the *Bā-mīn* of Malayalim. A most sporting fish. To be taken spinning in estuaries. Pages 198 to 210 of *The Rod in India*, where it is also figured.

Cybium Kuhlii.

B. vii, D. $16/\frac{5-6}{17-18}$ + viii, P. 29, V. 1/5, A. $\frac{4}{18}$ + vii, C. 21.

HABITAT.—Seas of India.

Cybium interruptum.

B. vii, D. $16/\frac{4}{15-16}$ + viii — ix, P. 21, V. 1/5, A. $\frac{2}{17}$ + viii—ix, C. 21.

HABITAT.—Seas of India. It attains at least 3 feet in length.

Cybium guttatum.

B. vii, D. $16-17/\frac{4-5}{14-15}$ + viii—x, P. 21, V. 1/5, A. $\frac{3}{17-19}$ + vii — ix, C. 26.

HABITAT.—Seas of India, Malay Archipelago, and China. Grows to 6 feet in length, is good eating, and salts well. Specimens under a foot in length are dry, from two to two-and-a-half feet long they are in the best condition, above that they become coarse. They should be cooked when quite fresh. They are also one of the best fish for "Tamarind-fish." Are captured in numbers from October throughout the cold months along all the Indian Coasts.

Cybium Commersonii.

Chumbum, Mal.; *Konam*, *Ma-wu-laachi*, or *Ah-ku-lah*, Tamil.

B. vii, D. 16 — 17/$\frac{3-4}{13-14}$ + ix — x, P. 20 — 23, V. 1/5, A. $\frac{2-3}{12-13}$ + ix — x, C. 21.

HABITAT.—Red sea, East Coast of Africa, seas of India to the Malay Archipelago and beyond; it attains at least 4 feet in length.

Cybium lineolatum.

B. vii, D. 16/$\frac{4}{12}$ + ix, P. 21, V. 1/5, A. $\frac{5}{14}$ + x, C. 15.

HABITAT.—Seas of India to ? Malay Archipelago.

All the *Cybii* are commonly known to Europeans as Seer fish. Attain at least 15 lbs. and I know not how much more. To be taken spinning. Page 214, *The Rod in India.*

Gobius giuris.

Wartee-poolah, *Pooan*, and *Kurdăn*, Mal.; *Nullatan Oolooway*, Tam.; *Tsikideondoa* and *Issakee doondoo*, Tel.; *Gulah*, Ooriah; *Nga-tha-boh*, Burmese; *Poo-dah*, Andam.; *Ab-bro-ny*, Canarese; *Goo-loo wah*, and *Boul-la*, Punj.; *Gooloo*, Sind and N. W. Provinces.

B. iv, D. 6/$\frac{1}{8-9}$, P. 20, V. 1/5, A. $\frac{1}{8-9}$, C. 17, L. l. 30—34, L. tr. 8—9, Vert. 11/16.

HABITAT.—East Coast of Africa, also in all pieces of fresh water throughout the plains of India, Ceylon, Burma, Sind, to the Malay Archipelago and beyond: attaining a foot and a half in length. This fish is much esteemed by the natives of India as being very light and wholesome, but unless elaborately cooked is not relished by Europeans because of its deficiency in, or earthy, taste. It is very voracious and takes a bait freely.

This is the Indian Gudgeon. See page 88 supra.

Mastacembelus armatus.

Bahm, *Vahm*, and *Gro-age*, Punj. and Sind.; *Kul-aral* and *Sha-ta-rah*, Tam.; *Mudi-bom-mi-day*, or "*Old Rhynchobdella*," Tel.; *Bahm*, *Bummi*, and *Gonti*, Ooriah and Beng.; *Nga-maway-doh-nga*, Burm.; "Thorny-backed eel."

B. vi, D. 32—39/74—90, P. 23, A. 3/75—88.

HABITAT.—This fish extends from Sind, throughout the fresh and brackish waters of the plains and hills of India, Ceylon, and Burma to China attaining two feet or more in length. It is good eating, especially when curried or fried.

To be taken like an eel on a dead fish. Fully treated in *The Rod in India*, page 187 and mentioned in pages 81 and 101 supra. If we spell the Tamil name *Ārāl* or *Kal-ārāl*, which is stone-ārāl we may recognize it more readily.

Ophiocephalus marulius.

Hoovina murl, Can.; *Pu verarl*, Tam.; *Pu murl*, Hind.; *Pula chapa*, Tel.; *Choaree-verarl* and *Curavu*, Mal.; *Kubrah*, *Sawl* and *Dowlah*, Punj.; *Nga-yan-dyne*, Burm.; *Ha-al*, Assam.

B. v, D. 45—55, P. 18, V. 6, A. 28—36, C. 14, L. l. 60—70, L. tr. $\frac{4\frac{1}{2}-6\frac{1}{2}}{13-11}$ or $\frac{5\frac{1}{2}-8\frac{1}{2}}{13-11}$.

Habitat.—Fresh waters, principally rivers, from Ceylon and India to China: attaining as much as four feet in length. Colonel Puckle observes "that they are very savage, protecting their young with great boldness." They take a live bait pretty well.

Ophiocephalus leucopunctatus.

B. v, D. 47—53, P. 18, V. 6, A. 28—35, C. 14, L. l. 59—60, L. tr. $\frac{4\frac{1}{2}-6\frac{1}{2}}{13-11}$ or $\frac{5-8}{13-11}$.

Habitat.—Coromandel and Western Coasts of India, also in some of the rivers of the Deccan: it appears to be found in China. It attains 3 feet or more in length.

Ophiocephalus barca.

B. v, D. 47—52, P. 16, V. 1/5, A. 34—36, C. 19, L. l. 60—65, L. tr. $\frac{5-6}{13}$.

Habitat.—Large rivers of the Bengal Presidency, portions of the North Western Provinces, and Assam. It attains three feet in length. "It inhabits perpendicular banks, in holes dug like those of the Martin (Hirundo). In these it lurks, watching for its prey, with its head out." (Ham. Buchanan.)

Ophiocephalus micropeltes.

B. v, D. 43—46, P. 15, V. 1/5, A. 27—30, C. 15, L. l. 95—110, L. tr. $\frac{7-8}{13-12}$, Vert. 53.

HABITAT.—Malabar and Western Coast of India, Siam to the Malay Archipelago. It attains at least three feet in length.

Ophiocephalus striatus.

Morrul, Murl, Dheri-murl, Hind.; *Sol* and *Chena*, Beng.; *Verarl* and *Wrahl*, Mal.; *Verarla* and *Currapu-verarl*, Tam.; *Sowarah*, Tel.; *Sola*, Ooriah; *Koochina-murl*, Canarese; *Loolla*, Singalese; *Nga-ain-di*, Mugh.

B. v, D. 37—45, P. 17, V. 6, A. 23—26, C. 13, L. l. 50—57, L. tr. $\frac{4\frac{1}{2}-7}{9-7}$ or $\frac{5\frac{1}{2}-8}{10-9}$, Vert. 13/39.

HABITAT.—Fresh waters throughout the plains of India, Ceylon, Burma, to China and the Philippines, especially delighting in swamps and grassy tanks: they attain 3 feet or more in length. They take a bait very readily, especially a frog, and are said to rise to the salmon fly.

Ophio-cephalus, the snake-headed or Marral is treated at length in *The Rod in India*, pages 174 to 186, and page 82 supra, and is figured in both books. The remarks are applicable to all the *Ophiocephalidæ* except *O. gachua* which is diminutive, and best suited for a bait, page 53 of *The Rod in India.*

Ophiocephalus gachua.

Dheri-dhok, Hind.; *Karavu*, Mal.; *Para korava*, Tam.; *Mah korava*, Can.; *Chenga* or *Chayung*, Ooriah; *Doarrah*, Punj.; *Chen-gah*, Assam.

B. v, D. 32—37, P. 15, V. 6, A. 21—23, C. 12, L. l. 40—45, L. tr. $\frac{3-4}{7-6}$.

HABITAT.—Fresh waters throughout India, Ceylon, Burma, and the Andamans, also near Gwadur on the Meckran Coast. This fish is often found thriving at the bottom of wells, and in fact may be taken from the waters of the plains to those in very high elevations. It attains at least 13 inches in length, is very voracious, and may often be captured in little watercourses, into which it has pursued the *Haplochili* and other small fish.

Etroplus Suratensis.

Karssar and *Pillinchan*, Tam.; *Pitul-kas*, Hind.; *Cashi-mara*, Telinga, (Jerdon); *Cundahla*, Ooriah; *Corallia*, Singalese (Boake).

B. vi, D. $\frac{18 - 19}{14 - 15}$, P. 17, V. 1/5, A. $\frac{12 - 13}{12 - 11}$, C. 16, L. l. 35—40, L. tr. 5½/17.

Habitat.—Fresh and brackish waters along the Coasts of Ceylon and India, as far as Orissa. Bloch named his fish received from the missionary John, Suratensis, on the supposition that it came from Surat. It does not appear however to be found in that locality, and more probably John obtained it at his station of Tranquebar where it is common. I have taken it inland in the Wynaad.

Page 90 supra.

Etroplus maculatus.

Pullattay, Mal.; *Rallia*, Singalese (Boake); *Boorakas* and *Chella kassu*, Tamil.

B. vi, D. $\frac{17 - 20}{8 - 10}$, P. 14, V. 1/5, A. $\frac{12 - 15}{8 - 9}$, C. 16, L. l. 35, L. tr. 6/19, Vert. 15/13.

Habitat.—Fresh waters along the Coasts of Madras, and from South Canara along Malabar, and also found in Ceylon. It is captured at least sixty or eighty miles inland.

Page 92 supra.

Macrones aor.

Mukul-jellah, Tel.; *Cumboo Kelletee*, Tam.; *Nga-joung*, Burm.; *Seengala* and *Sang-go-ah*, Punj.; *Singharee*, Sind.; *Alli* or *Addi*, Ooriah.

B. xii, D. 1/0, P. 1/9—10, V. 6, A. 12—13 $\left(\frac{3-4}{9}\right)$, C. 17.

Habitat.—Throughout Sind and India to Burma, a specimen in Calcutta is 3 feet long.

Probably to be taken in the same way as *Macrones seengala*.

Macrones seenghala.

Teng ga-ra, Punj.

B. xii, D. 1/0, P. 1/9, V. 6, A. 11—12 $\left(\frac{3}{8-9}\right)$, C. 19—21.

Habitat.—The Indus, salt ranges of the Punjab, Jumna and Ganges, certainly as low as Delhi, also the Deccan, Kistna river to its termination, and Assam. It attains a considerable size.

Page 79 supra.

Macrones punctatus.

Sholang kellete, Tamil.

B. xi, D. $\frac{1}{7}$/0, P. 1/7, V. 6, A. 11—13 $\left(\frac{3-4}{8-9}\right)$, C. 17.

HABITAT.—Bowany river at base of Neilgherry hills, attaining at least 18 inches in length.

Probably to be taken like *Macrones seenghala* or *Callichrous bimaculatus.*

Macrones cavasius.

Vella kelletee and *Cutta*, Tam.; *Muti jella*, Tel.; *Guntea*, Ooriah; *Kavasi tengara*, Beng.; *Nya-zin-zine*, Burmese.

B. vi, D. $\frac{1}{7}$/0, P. 1/8, V. 6, A. 11—13 $\left(\frac{4}{7-9}\right)$, C. 16.

HABITAT.—From Sind, throughout India, Assam, and Burma: attaining at least 18 inches in length.

Probably to be taken like other *Macrones* or like *Callichrous bimaculatus.*

Callichrous bimaculatus.

Dūka-dūmū, Tel.; *Godla*, Canarese; *Dimmon*, Sind.; *Chotah-wahlah*, Tam.; *Pob-tah*, Ooriah; *Pah-boh*, Assam.; *Pufta*, *Goongwah*, and *Pallu*, Punj.; *Goong-wah-ree* and *Puf-ta*, N. W. Provinces.

B. xii, D. 4, P. 1/13, V. 8, A. 60—75 $\left(\frac{2-3}{58-72}\right)$, C. 17.

HABITAT.—The fresh waters of Sind, and from the Punjab throughout India, Ceylon, and Assam to the Malay Archipelago and beyond. It attains at least a foot-and-a-half in length.

Page 86 supra.

Callichrous Malabaricus.

Mungee Wahlah, Mal.

B. xv, D. 4, P. 1/13—14, V. 8, A. 61—69 $\left(\frac{3}{58-66}\right)$, C. 17.

HABITAT.—Malabar Coast of India up to 20 inches in length.

Probably to be taken like *Callichrous bimaculatus.*

Wallago attu.

Wah-lah, Mal. and Tam.; *Mul-la* and *Pi-i-kee* and *Jer-i-kee*, Sind.; *Boyari*, Beng.

B. xix—xxi, D. 5, P. 1/13—15, V. 8—10, A. 86—93 $\left(\frac{4}{82-89}\right)$, C. 17, Vert. 13/56.

HABITAT.—Throughout India, Ceylon and Burma. It attains at least six feet in length, and is good eating, but is a voracious and not very cleanly feeder. A stuffed specimen in Calcutta is 4½ feet long.

Page 72 supra and pages 167 to 169, *The Rod in India*. Figured in both books.

Silundia Gangetica.

Silond, Punj.; *Jil-lung* and *Silond*, Ooriah and Beng., *Wanjou*, Telugu.

B. xi—xii, D. $\frac{1}{7}$/0, P. 1/11—13, V. 6, A. 40—46 $\left(\frac{4}{36-44}\right)$, C. 17.

HABITAT.—Estuaries of India and Burma, ascending high up the larger rivers to nearly their sources. It attains 6 feet or more in length, and is called "a shark" by the natives. It is very voracious.

Page 170 *The Rod in India*, and page 78 supra.

Bagarius Yarrellii.

Boonch or *Goonch*, Hind. (N. W. P.); *Goreah*, Assam.; *Rahti jellah*, Tel.; *Sah-lun*, Ooriah.

B. xii, D. $\frac{1}{6}$/0, P. 1/12, V. 6, A. 13 — 15 $\left(\frac{3}{10-12}\right)$, C. 17.

HABITAT.—Large rivers of India and Java, descending to the estuaries. It attains 6 feet or more in length, and is often termed a "freshwater shark," partly due to its voracity, and partly to its underhung mouth and general ugliness.

Page 169 *The Rod in India*, and page 78 supra.

Labeo fimbriatus.

Ven-kendai, Tam.; *Ruchu* and *Gandumenu*, Tel.; *Bahrum*, Ooriah.

B. iii, D. 19·22 $\left(\frac{3-4}{15-18}\right)$, P. 17, V. 9, A. 7 ($\frac{2}{5}$), C. 19, L. l. 44—47, L. tr. 9—10/8.

HABITAT.—Sind, Punjab, the Deccan, and probably N. E. Bengal; also Southern India at least to Orissa. Not recorded from Malabar or

Canara. It attains a foot and half in length, and is good eating, but bony.

I think this is more correctly *Shēl-kendai* in Tamil. *Veng-kendai* is *Cirrhina cirrhosa*. Chapter I of this book.

Labeo nigrescens.

Mul-vel and *Kurri-minu*, Canarese.

B. iii, D. 17 — 18 $\left(\frac{2-3}{14-15}\right)$, P. 19, A. 7 $(\frac{2}{5})$, C. 19 — 21, L. l. 36, L. tr. 6/7.

HABITAT.—Mangalore and South Canara. It is said to attain 18 inches in length.

Probably to be taken like the other Labeo.

Labeo calbasu.

Nulla-gandu-menu, Telugu; *Kalbasu* and *Kundna*, Beng. and *Cuggera* (Soane); *Mahlee*, Assam.; *Kalabeinse*, Ooriah and Hind.; *Di*, Punj.; *Di-hee*, Sind.; *Dai*, Cutch; *Kurri-minu*, Canarese; *Nga-nek-pya*, *Nga-noo-than*, and *Nga-ong-tong*, Burmese.

B. iii, D. 16 — 18 $\left(\frac{3}{13-15}\right)$, P. 19, V. 9, A. 7 $(\frac{2}{5})$, C. 19, L. l. 40–44, L. tr. 7½/8.

HABITAT.—Punjab, Sind, Cutch, Deccan, Southern India and Malabar, from the Kistna through Orissa, Bengal and Burma. It grows to 3 feet in length: were it not for its numerous bones, it would be excellent eating.

This is the Kāla-bous of Northern India. *Shēl-kendai* of Tamil. Chapter I of this book.

Labeo gonius.

Mosoo, Tel.; *Cursua*, Ooriah; *Kurchi* and *Goni*, Beng.; *Cursa* and *Colloose*, Hind.; *Courie* and *Bahtoor*, Assam.; *Cir-re-oh*, Sind.; *Nga-pay*, Tennass.; *Nga-dane*, and *Nga-hoo*, Burmese.

B iii, D. 16 — 18 $\left(\frac{2-3}{13-14}\right)$, P. 17, V. 9, A. 7 $(\frac{2}{5})$, C. 19, L. l. 74—84, L. tr. 16/17.

HABITAT.—Indus in Sind, through the N. W. Provinces, Bengal, and Orissa to Ganjam, as low as the Kistna: Assam and Burma. It attains nearly 5 feet in length.

Presumably to be taken like other Labeo, as described in Chapter I of this book.

Labeo rohita.

Ruhu, Ooriah ; *Ruee*, Beng. ; *Nga-myit-chin* and *Nga-myit-tsan-nee*, Burmese ; *Dum-bra*, Sind.

B. iii, D. 15 — 16 $\left(\frac{3}{12-13}\right)$, P. 17, V. 9, A. 7 ($\frac{2}{5}$), C. 19, L. l. 40 — 42, L. tr. 6½/9.

HABITAT.—Fresh waters of Sind, and from the Punjab through India and Assam to Burma. It is not found in Madras or the Western Coast. It attains 3 feet or more in length. It is esteemed excellent as food, and propagated with care in ponds in Bengal.

Pages 50 and 62 to 65 supra.

Labeo Kontius.

Currumunnee candee and *Curoo-moolee-candee*, Tam.

B. iii, D. 15 — 16 $\left(\frac{3-4}{12-13}\right)$, P. 15, V. 10, A. 7 ($\frac{2}{5}$), C. 19, L. l. 38 — 41, L. tr. 7/8.

HABITAT.—Rivers along the base of the Neilgherries, and the Cauvery and Coleroon in all their branches down to the Coast. It grows to two feet in length.

Another local name of this fish is *Gundumani-shēl-kendai*, from its having a red and black eye like the seed of the *Abrus precatorius* (Country Liquorice bush). It grows to 20 lbs. in weight. Chapter I, supra.

Labeo dyocheilus.

Boalla, Hind. ; *Heel-gorya*, Assamese ; *Nu-ga-dee*, Sind.

B. iii, D. 13 ($\frac{3}{11}$), P. 17, V. 9, A. 7 ($\frac{2}{5}$), C. 19, L. l. 43, L. tr. 8½/7½.

HABITAT.—Scind hills and along the Himalayas to Sikkim and Assam. It is common in Assam. It attains at least 3 feet in length.

Presumably to be taken like other Labeo. Chapter I, supra.

Labeo bata.

Dunguda-porah, Ooriah ; *Dommarci-batta*, Beng. ; *Gootellah*, Hind. ; *Bango*, N. W. Provinces ; *Tchirri*, Cutch.

B. iii, D. 11 — 12 $\left(\frac{2-3}{9-10}\right)$ P. 18, V. 9, A. 7 ($\frac{2}{5}$), C. 19, L. l. 37 — 40, L. tr. 7/6 — 7.

HABITAT.—From the Kistna and Godavery rivers, through Orissa,

Lower Bengal, and Assam. This fish (which attains nearly two feet in length) is extensively used for stocking tanks.

About the Labeo generally see the whole of the first chapter of this book and specially pages 2 and 14.

Cirrhina cirrhosa.

Ven-candi, Tam.; *Aruzu*, Telugu.

B. iii, D. 17—19 $\left(\frac{3-4}{14-15}\right)$, P. 19, V. 9, A. 8 ($\frac{2}{5}$), C. 19, L. l. 42—44, L. tr. 8/9, Vert. 21/17.

HABITAT.—Godavery, Kistna and Cauvery rivers, and generally in Southern India. Grows to $1\frac{1}{2}$ feet in length. Is a very active fish and fair eating, but bony.

I would write the Tamil name *Veng-kendai*, which means White Carp. Pages 5 and 46 supra.

Cirrhina mrigala.

Mirrgah, Ooriah; *Mrigala*, Bengali and Hind.; *Naim*, Hind. (N. W. P.); *Nga-kyin* and *Nga-gyein*, Burm.; *Mor-ah-kee*, Sind and Cutch.

B. iii, D. 15—16 $\left(\frac{3}{12-13}\right)$, P. 15, V. 9, A. 8 ($\frac{3}{5}$), C. 15, L. l. 40—45, L. tr. $6\frac{1}{2}$—$7/8\frac{1}{2}$.

HABITAT.—Rivers and tanks in Bengal, Deccan, N. W. Provinces, Punjab, Sind, Cutch, and Burma, growing to 3 feet in length. It is an excellent species for stocking tanks with. I have taken it in Rangoon 18 pounds in weight.

Pages 46 and 104 supra.

Cirrhina reba.

Eelemose and *Chittahri*, Tel.; *Chetchua-porah*, Ooriah; *Batta*, Bengali; *Rewah*, Hind.; *Soonnee*, Punj. and Sind.; *Lasseem*, Assam.

B. iii, D. 10—11 $\left(\frac{2-3}{8-9}\right)$, P. 16, V. 9, A. 8 ($\frac{2}{5}$), C. 19, L. l. 35—38, L. tr. 7/9.

HABITAT.—Throughout India, attaining a foot in length.

Probably to be taken like the Cirrhina cirrhosa, or White Carp.

Catla Buchanani.

Botchee, Telugu; *Catla*, Beng., Hind. and Punj.; *Barkur*, Ooriah;

Nga-thaing, Burmese; *Tambra*, Hind. in Bombay; *Boassa*, Hind. in N. W. Provinces; *Tay-lee*, Sind.

B. iii, D. 17–19 $\left(\frac{3-4}{14-16}\right)$, P. 21, V. 9, A. 8 ($\frac{3}{5}$), C. 19, L. l. 40–43, L. tr. 7½/9, Vert. 17/18.

HABITAT.—Sind, Punjab, through India to the Kistna, and eastwards through Bengal, and Burma to Siam. It attains at least 6 feet in length, and is much esteemed as food when not exceeding 2 feet, larger ones are coarse. It resides in fresh or brackish water, being found within tidal influence. "It is a very strong active animal, and often leaps over the seine of the fishermen, on which account, when fishing for the *Catla*, they usually follow the net in canoes, and make a noise by shouting and splashing with their paddles." (Ham. Buchanan). It is said never to take a bait, but as it rises at natural flies, it could probably be taken with artificial ones.

Pages 51 and 104 supra.

Barbus sarana.

Pungella, Tam.; *Giddi-kaoli*, *Durhie* and *Potah*, Hind.; *Gid-pakke*, Can.; *Kannaku*, Tel.; *Sarana*, Ooriah and Beng.; *Jundoori*, Punj.; *Pop-pree* and *Kuh-nah-nee*, Sind.; *Sen-nee*, Assam.; *Nga-khon-mah-gyee* and *Nga-chong*, Burmese.

B. iii, D. 11 ($\frac{3}{8}$), P. 15, V. 9, A. 8 ($\frac{3}{5}$), C. 19, L. l. 32–34, L. tr. 5½–6/6.

HABITAT.—Sind and the Punjab, throughout India, Assam and Burma, in which latter country the caudal fin has sometimes a black upper and lower edge and a dark mark at the base of each scale. It attains at least a foot in length.

Pages 49 and 50 supra.

Barbus chrysopoma.

Munduttee, Mal.

B. iii, D. 12 ($\frac{4}{8}$), P. 17, V. 9, A. 8 ($\frac{3}{5}$), C. 19, L. l. 28–30, L. tr. 6/6.

HABITAT.—Fresh waters along the Coasts of India from Cutch to Bengal, also the Deccan, Mysore, and Madras. I have likewise received it from Darjeeling.

Pages 37, 49 and 50 supra.

Barbus Carnaticus.

Poaree candee, *Saal candee*, *Shellee*, Tamil; *Giddi-kaoli*, Hind.; *Gid-pakke*, Can.

B. iii, D. 12 ($\frac{4}{8}$), P. 15, V. 9, A. 7 ($\frac{2}{5}$), C. 19, L. l. 32, L. tr. 5/6.

HABITAT.—Rivers along the bases of the Neilgherries, Wynaad, and

South Canara hills. It attains at least 25 lbs. in weight. Some have been introduced into the Ootacamund lake.

The Rod in India, pages 118 to 139.

Barbus hexagonolepis.

Bokar and *Boolooah*, Assam.

B. iii, D. 12 ($\frac{3}{9}$), P. 17, V. 9, A. 7 ($\frac{2}{5}$), C. 19, L. l. 28—31, L. tr. $4\frac{1}{2}/4\frac{1}{2}$.

HABITAT.—Assam in the larger rivers, and those from the Himalayas. It attains upwards of 2 feet in length, and takes a fly or bait freely.

Probably to be taken like *Barbus Carnaticus.*

Barbus Dukai.

B. iii, D. 13 ($\frac{4}{9}$), P. 15, V. 9, A. 7 ($\frac{2}{5}$), C. 19, L. l. 28—29, L. tr. 4/4.

HABITAT.—Teesta river, Darjeeling, from whence Dr. Duka sent me several examples, and after whom I have named it.

I have taken it in the Jaldoka a tributary of the Teesta, just as I would Carnatic Carp.

Barbus tor.

Burapatra, Assam.; *Poo-meen-candee*, Tam.; *Naharm*, Hind.; *Kukhiah*, Punj.; *Joon-gah*, *Petiah* and *Kurreah*, Sind.

B. iii, D. 12 ($\frac{3}{9}$), P. 19, V. 9, A. 7—8$\left(\frac{2-3}{5}\right)$, L. l. 25—27, L. tr. 4/4.

HABITAT.—Generally throughout India, but in the largest size, and greatest abundance in mountain streams or those which are rocky.

This is the mighty Mahseer for which see "*The Rod in India.*"

Barbus hexastichus.

Lobura, Assam.

B. iii, D. 12—13$\left(\frac{3-4}{9}\right)$, P. 17, V. 9, A. 7 ($\frac{2}{5}$), C. 19, L. l. 25—26, L. tr. 4/5.

HABITAT.—Rivers on and around Himalayas, Cashmere, Sikhim and Assam, growing to 3 feet in length. Specimens from the plains appear to have the head comparatively longer than those from the hills. Ceylon examples, which seem to be a variety, have a longer dorsal spine, it being equal to or a little longer than the head.

Probably to be taken like Mahseer or Carnatic Carp.

Barbus curmuca.

B. iii, D. 12 ($\frac{3}{9}$), P. 16, V. 9, A. 8 ($\frac{3}{5}$), C. 18, L. l. 41, L. tr. 8/7.

HABITAT.—Western Ghauts of India, attaining to at least 4 feet in length. Jerdon obtained it from Palghaut and Arriacode in South Malabar.

I have taken these like Carnatic Carp.

Barbus lithopidos.

Kuri meen, Canarese.

B. iii, D. 12 ($\frac{3}{9}$), P. 15, V. 10, A. 8 ($\frac{3}{5}$), C. 19, L. l. 38—39, L. tr. 7/7.

HABITAT.—South Canara, where it is not uncommon in the rivers, and attains 2 feet in length.

I have taken them like Carnatic Carp spinning a small spoon.

Barbus Thomassi.

Kem-pu-per-ru-wul, Canarese (Red Mahaseer).

B. iii, D. 12—13 $\left(\frac{3—4}{9}\right)$, P. 17, V. 10, A. 8 ($\frac{3}{5}$), C. 19, L. l. 31—34, L. tr. 6/6.

HABITAT.—South Canara, attaining at least 3½ feet in length. I have named the species after Mr. H. S. Thomas, M.C.S., who first brought the fish to my notice.

The mouth is not so large comparatively as that of the ordinary Mahseer, *Barbus tor*, and I should doubt their taking a spinning bait. Bottom fishing as for Labeo would probably succeed better. I have only seen them caught with a net. They are a most handsome fish, being of a deep pink all over and are large fish.

Barbus Jerdoni.

Say-meen, Can.; *Cha-meen*, Tulu.; *Ta-meen*, Mal.

B. iii, D. 12 ($\frac{3}{9}$), P. 15, V. 9, A. 8 ($\frac{3}{5}$), C. 19, L. l. 27—28, L. tr. 6/4.

HABITAT.—Rivers in Canara below the Ghauts attaining 18 inches in length.

This is a deep set and most beautiful fish, the body being bright like silver in strong contrast with brilliant deep vermillion fins, from which I wanted to have named it *Barbus rododactylos.* But there is already a *Barbus rodactylus*, and it was just at the time of Jerdon's death that I gave it to Dr. Day, and so the fish got named *in memoriam* of the great naturalist. The Canara rivers teem with this beautiful fish, which in all its habits is the local equivalent of the Carnatic Carp, as *Barbus Dukai* is in the Teesta and Jaldoka, and probably elsewhere northwards, though only recorded from those two rivers as yet. This rosy-fingered beauty was too much for me in my early fishing days in Canara, but since I have found out how to tackle the Carnatic Carp I am confident this beautiful fish (*Sē-mīn* in Canarese) might be taken in exactly the same way. In my early days I never fished the stiller waters which it affects in shoals, spinning only in the rougher runs for Mahseer. It is only recorded from Canara, but it is probably spread up and down the West Coast.

Barbus Neilli.

B. iii, D. 13 ($\frac{4}{9}$), P. 15, V. 10, A. 8 ($\frac{3}{5}$), C. 19, L. l. 24—26, L. tr. $4\frac{1}{2}$/4.

HABITAT.—Kurnool on the Tamboodra river. The largest specimen personally seen was 38 lbs. weight, but it is said to attain to 50 or 60 lbs.

It is probably to be taken just like a Mahseer. There are many different fish that pass as Mahseer. I have seen at least three in a single river and many more in others.

Barbus Malabaricus.

B. iii, D. 12—13 $\left(\frac{3-4}{9}\right)$, P. 17, V. 9, A. 8 ($\frac{3}{5}$), C. 19, L. l. 24, L. tr. 4/4.

HABITAT.—From South Canara down the Western Ghauts to the Travancore hills. Mr. Ballard has captured it at Courtallum with a fly. It attains at least 18 inches in length.

Barbus Mahecola.

B. iii, D. 11 ($\frac{3}{8}$), P. 15, V. 9, A. 7 ($\frac{2}{5}$), C. 19, L. l. 21, L. tr. 5/4.

HABITAT.—From Canara down the Western Coast and along the base of the Neilgherries, and Travancore hills, also Ceylon. It attains at least 6 inches in length.

To be taken with a fly. Runs ordinarily a quarter of a pound. *Rod in India*, page 144.

Barbus filamentosus.

B. iii, D. 11 ($\frac{3}{8}$), P. 15, V. 9, A. 7 ($\frac{2}{5}$), C. 19, L. l. 21, L. tr. 4/4.

HABITAT.—Western Coast and Southern India, attaining 6 inches in length. It is so similar to *B. Mahecola* (excepting in wanting barbels) that I have not figured it.

To be taken like *Barbus Mahecola*. *Rod in India*, page 144, where it is figured and colored.

Barilius Bakeri.

B. iii, D. 13 ($\frac{3}{10}$), P. 15, V. 9, A. 16—17$\left(\frac{2-3}{14}\right)$, C. 17, L. l. 38, L. tr. 9/4.

HABITAT.—Hill ranges of Travancore, whence I received several specimens collected by the Revd. H. Baker. It attains 6 inches in length.

All these Barils are to be taken with a fly. See *Rod in India*, pages 147 to 157.

Barilius gatensis.

Choares (at Coonoor) and *Aart-candee* (Bowany), Tamil, "River Carp."

B. iii, D. 10—12$\left(\frac{2-3}{8-9}\right)$, P. 15, V. 9, A. 15—17$\left(\frac{3}{12-14}\right)$, C. 18, L. l. 39—40, L. tr. 8/5.

HABITAT.—Western Ghauts of Malabar and Neilgherry hills, up to about 5,000 feet above the level of the sea. It attains at least 6 inches in length.

This is the Baril with which the Kodi-kānal Lake on the Pulney Hills, Madura District, is stocked full. I have taken 7 dozen in a forenoon with a fly. The best months are March to June after which they spawn and fall off. They are said to come on again in October.

Barilius Canarensis.

B. iii, D. 12—13$\left(\frac{2}{10-11}\right)$, P. 15, V. 9, A. 14—16$\left(\frac{2}{12-14}\right)$, C. 21, L. l. 38, L. tr. 9/4.

HABITAT.—Canara and Malabar on the Western Coast; attaining 6 inches in length.

I have taken these with a fly as described in *The Rod in India.*

Barilius guttatus.

Nga-la-wah, Burm.

B. iii, D. 9 ($\frac{2}{7}$), P. 15, V. 9, A. 14 ($\frac{3}{11}$), C. 17, L. l. 44—48, L. tr. 9/5.

HABITAT.—Irrawaddi from Prome to Mandalay; attaining at least 7 inches in length.

Probably to be taken with a fly just like the others.

Barilius bola.

Bugguah, Ooriah; *Korang*, Assam.; *Bola*, Beng.; *Buggarah*, Hind.

B. iii, D. 10—11$\left(\frac{3}{7-8}\right)$, P. 13, V. 9, A. 13 ($\frac{3}{10}$), C. 19, L. l. 88—94, L. tr. 12—15/9—11.

HABITAT.—Orissa, Bengal, N. W. Provinces, Assam and Burma, attaining at least a foot in length: one killed in Assam by Mr. Hannay, is stated to have weighed 5 lbs. It is a very game fish, takes the fly well, and is one of those termed Rajah mas, or "chief of the fishes" in the Assam rivers.

Commonly called the Indian trout. Page 154 of *The Rod in India* where it is figured. It ought to be introduced to our Hill Lakes. I have taken it spinning and fly fishing.

Chela gora.

Hum-catchari, Ooriah; *Ghora chela*, Beng.; *Chel-hul*, Hind.; *Bounchi* and *Kundul*, Punj.

B. iii, D. 9—10$\left(\frac{2-3}{7}\right)$, P. 15, V. 8, A. 15—16$\left(\frac{2}{13-14}\right)$, C. 19, L. l. 140—160, L. tr. 18—20/18, Vert. 46.

HABITAT.—Sind, Punjab, N. W. Provinces, Bengal, Orissa, and Assam. It attains at least 9 inches in length.

Probably to be taken with a fly like all the other Chela or Chilwa as mentioned in *The Rod in India* and probably also with a float as indicated, page 93 supra.

Chela sardinella.

Nga-koon-nyat, Burm.

B. iii, D. 9 $(\frac{2}{7})$, P. 13, V. 8, A. 21 $(\frac{3}{18})$, L. l. 48, L. tr. 7½/4.

HABITAT.—Irrawaddi river at Rangoon, also the Salwein at Moulmein. It attains to at least 6 inches in length.

See *Chela gora.*

Chela untrahi.

Untrahi, Ooriah.

B. iii, D. 9 $(\frac{2}{7})$, P. 13, V. 7, A. 17—19$\left(\frac{2-3}{14-17}\right)$, C. 17, L. l. 55—65, L. tr. 7—9/5.

HABITAT.—Mahanuddi river in Orissa, also the Cauvery and Coleroon in Southern India. It attains at least eight inches in length.

See *Chela gora.*

Chela argentea.

Chaya-vellachee or *Vellachee-cundee*, Tam., "The White Carp."

B. iii, D. 9—10$\left(\frac{2-3}{7-8}\right)$, P. 15, V. 8, A. 17—19$\left(\frac{3}{14-16}\right)$, C. 19, L. l. 43—45, L. tr. 6½—7/3.

HABITAT.—Bowany river at the base of the Neilgherries, Cauvery river and Mysore attaining 6 inches in length.

The ordinary name in Tamil is *Velachi*, dropping the *kendai*, which is the lax generic name for Carp. It is not properly translateable, White Carp but Silver Carp. I only mention it to avoid confusion with *Veng-kendai* which is White Carp. Europeans commonly call this fish the silver fish. For its capture, see *Rod in India* and page 93 supra.

Chela boopis.

B. iii, D. 9—10$\left(\frac{2-3}{7}\right)$, P. 15, V. 9, A. 14—15$\left(\frac{2-3}{12-13}\right)$, C. 21, L. l. 38—40, L. tr. 6—6½/3.

HABITAT.—South Canara and ? Mysore; attaining at least 5 inches in length.

I have taken it like *C. argentea.*

Chela clupeoides.

Netteli, Tam.

B. iii, D. 9 $(\frac{2}{7})$, P. 13, V. 9, A. 13—15 $\left(\frac{2}{11-13}\right)$, C. 19, L. l. 80—93, L. tr. 12—15/6.

HABITAT.—Cutch, Jubbulpore, Mysore, the Deccan, Madras Presidency, and Burma. It attains at least 6 inches in length, and is very good eating.

I have taken it like *C. argentea.*

Chela bacaila.

Jellahri, Ooriah; *Chelliah*, Hind.

B. iii, D. 9 $(\frac{2}{7})$, P. 13, V. 9, A. 13—15 $\left(\frac{2}{11-13}\right)$, C. 19, L. l. 86—110, L. tr. 17—19/6—10.

HABITAT.—Throughout India except Malabar, Mysore, and Madras, and parts of the Deccan. Dr. Günther gives Moulmein as one of its localities. It attains at least 7 inches in length.

See *C. gora.*

Clupea ilisha.

"Sable fish" and "Hilsa" of Europeans; *Palasah*, Tel.; *Pulla*, Sind.; *Oolum*, Tamil; *Nga-tha-louk*, Burmese; *Hilsa*, Beng.

B. vi, D. 18—19 $\left(\frac{3}{15-16}\right)$, P. 15, V. 9, A. 19—22 $\left(\frac{2}{17-20}\right)$, C. 19, L. l. 46—49, L. tr. 17—19, Vert. 12/32—34.

HABITAT.—Persian Gulf ascending the Tigris, the Coasts of Sind, India, and Burma, passing up the large rivers to breed, also the Malay Archipelago. I have taken them as high as Delhi, and Hamilton Buchanan records them from Agra and Cawnpore.

An angler told me he had taken them with a white fly. They are a sea fish ascending rivers like salmon, for the purpose of spawning in fresh water.

Elops saurus.

Jallugu and *Jinnagow*, Tel.; *Ullahti*, Tamil.

B. xxix—xxxv, D. 22—24 $\left(\frac{4}{18-20}\right)$, P. 19, V. 6, A. 15—17 $\left(\frac{3-4}{12-13}\right)$, C. 19, L. l. 95—100, L. tr. 12/14.

HABITAT.—Red Sea, East Coast of Africa, through the seas of India to the Malay Archipelago and beyond. It attains a considerable length.

This is an estuary fish. It is to be taken like *Megalops* on a small spinning bait or a white fly. It is astonishingly active. There are plenty in the Madras Fort moat. The Tamil name is more correctly *Ālătti*. *Rod in India*, page 214.

Megalops cyprinoides.

Punnikowu and *Naharn*, Ooriah ; *Cunnay*, Mal. ; *Mordu cundai*, Tamil ; *Nga-tan-youet*, Burmese.

B. xxiv—xxvi, D. 19—21 $\left(\frac{2}{17-19}\right)$, P. 15—16, V. 10, A. 24—27 $\left(\frac{2}{22-25}\right)$, C. 19, L. l. 37—42, L. tr. 5—6/6.

HABITAT.—East Coast of Africa, fresh waters and estuaries of India, Ceylon, Malay Archipelago, China, and Polynesia. It is occasionally captured in rivers, but much more commonly found in tanks.

It is an estuary fish easily accommodating itself to fresh water, on which account it is much affected by Mahomedans who get fry caught in the estuaries and put them in their tanks. I have seen them a cubit long and taken them spinning. *The Rod in India*, page 214, where also it is figured. The Tamil name is more correctly *Morăng kendai*. Page 87 supra.

Chanos salmoneus.

Tulu candal, Tam. ; *Palah bontah*, Tel. ; *Hu-meen*, Can. ; *Pu-meen*, Tulu.

B. iv, D. 13—16 $\left(\frac{2-4}{11-12}\right)$, P. 16, V. 11, A. 9—10 $\left(\frac{2-3}{7}\right)$, C. 19, L. l. 80—90, L. tr. 12/15, Vert. 19—26.

HABITAT.—Red Sea, seas of India to the Malay Archipelago and beyond. Attains 3 feet at least in length: is called the *milk fish* or *white mullet* by Europeans in South Canara, where Hyder Ali introduced it from the sea into tanks of fresh and brackish water where it still thrives.

It is mentioned in *The Rod in India*, page 217, as not to be taken with a rod and line that I then knew of, but a prawn, dead and skinned as described, page 89 supra, is found to fetch him. This fish is an estuary fish which readily acclimatises itself to fresh water and can be netted with no great difficulty in the estuaries as fry.

Notopterus kapirat.

Moh, *But* and *Purri*, Punj.; *Moh*, N. W. Prov.; *Pholoe*, Beng.; *Ambutan-wahlah* or "*Barber's knife*" and *Chota wahlah*, Tam.; *Wallak-tattah*, Mysore; *Pulli* or 'a slice,' Ooriah; *Kan-doo-lee*, Assam.; *Nga-hpeh* and *Nga-phe*, Burm.

B. viii, D. 7—8 $\left(\frac{1-2}{6-7}\right)$, P. 17, V. 5—6, A. 100—110, C. 19, L. r. 225, Vert. 15/54.

Habitat.—Fresh and brackish waters of India to the Malay Archipelago. Grow to 2 feet or more in length.

See page 87 supra.

Notopterus chitala.

Chitul, Ooriah; *See-tul*, Assam.; *Gundun*, Sind.; *Chitala*, Beng.

B. viii—ix, D. 9—10 $\left(\frac{1-2}{7-9}\right)$, P. 16, V. 6, A. 110—125 (135), C. 12—14, L. l. 180, Cæc. pyl. 2.

Habitat.—Fresh waters of Sind, Lower Bengal, Orissa, Assam, Burma, and Siam to the Malay Archipelago. It attains at least 4 feet in length.

Page 87 supra.

Anguilla Bengalensis.

B. xii, D. 250—305, P. 18, A. 220—250, C. 10—12.

Habitat.—Islands in the Indian Ocean, continent of India and Burma. It is common at the Andaman Islands. It probably extends its range to the Malay Archipelago, Formosa and the Pacific. It attains four feet and upwards in length and is much rarer on the hills than in the plains. Some have been introduced into the waters on the Neilgherry hills in Madras.

Rod in India, page 187 and page 81 supra.

INDEX.